Counselling problem drinkers

D1135762

Edited by
Robin Davidson, Stephen Rollnick
and Ian MacEwan

on behalf of the
New Directions in the Study of Alcohol Group

Tavistock/Routledge
London and New York

First published in 1991
by Routledge
11 New Fetter Lane, London EC4P 4EE
Simultaneously published in the USA and Canada
by Routledge
a division of Routledge, Chapman and Hall Inc.
29 West 35th Street, New York, NY 10001

Reprinted 1992

© 1991 Robin Davidson, Stephen Rollnick and Ian MacEwan
Typeset by Witwell Ltd, Southport
Printed in England by Clays Ltd, St Ives plc

British Library Cataloguing in Publication Data
Counselling problem drinkers.
   1. Great Britain. Welfare work with alcoholics
   I. Davidson, Robin, *1950–* II. Rollnick, Stephen, *1952–*
   III. MacEwan, Ian, *1949–* IV. New Directions in the Study
   of Alcohol Group
   362.29280941

Library of Congress Cataloging in Publication Data
   Counselling problem drinkers/edited on behalf of the New Directions
   in the Study of Alcohol Group by Robin Davidson, Stephen Rollnick,
   and Ian MacEwan.
     p.   cm.
   Includes bibliographical references and index.
   1. Alcoholism counseling. 2. Alcoholics—Rehabilitation.
   I. Davidson, Robin, M. Sc., M. Sc. (Clin. Psych.), ABPS.
   II. Rollnick, Stephen, 1952– . III. MacEwan, Ian, 1949– .
   IV. New Directions in the Study of Alcohol Group (Great Britain)
   HV5276.C68 1990   90–8619
   362.29′286—dc20

ISBN 0–415–03160–5

Contents

v

Contents

Figures and tables

Figures

Tables

Contributors

Steven Allsop was formerly a lecturer in the Alcohol Studies Centre, Paisley College of Technology, Scotland, and is now Director of Education and Research for the Alcohol and Drug Authority of Western Australia.

Steve Baldwin is Consultant Clinical Psychologist and co-ordinator of the TACADE Neighbourhood Networks Project in Manchester. He is also Visiting Research Fellow at the Polytechnic Southwest, Plymouth, England.

Ken Barrie trained as a social worker and is now Director of the Alcohol Studies Centre, Paisley College of Technology, Scotland.

Robin Davidson is Area Clinical Psychologist, Northern Health and Social Services Board and Honorary Lecturer at the Queen's University of Belfast, Northern Ireland.

Nick Heather is Professor of Alcohol Studies and Director of the National Drug and Alcohol Research Centre, University of New South Wales, Sydney, Australia.

Ian MacEwan is a social worker who formerly worked with Alcohol Concern and is now Manager of the Alcohol Liquor Advisory Council, New Zealand.

Duncan Raistrick is Consultant Psychiatrist at the Leeds Addiction Unit, and Honorary Lecturer at the University of Leeds, England.

Stephen Rollnick is Clinical Psychologist at Whitchurch Hospital, Cardiff, Wales and Visiting Research Fellow at the National Drug and Alcohol Research Centre, University of New South Wales, Sydney, Australia.

Bill Saunders was formerly Director of the Alcohol Studies Centre, Paisley College of Technology, Scotland, and is now Associate Professor and Director of the Addiction Studies Unit, Curtin University, Perth, Western Australia.

Moyra Sidell is Research Fellow for the Open University, Milton Keynes, England.

Gillian Tober trained as a social worker and is now Tutor in Addictions at the Leeds Addiction Unit, England.

Foreword

Nick Heather

It is a pleasure and a privilege to be asked to write a foreword for the second book produced by the New Directions in the Study of Alcohol Group. On this occasion, the editors have chosen to compile a book of immediate practical value to the alcohol counsellor and also to structure it around Prochaska and DiClemente's model of the stages of change process, both highly commendable decisions.

I first became aware of the Prochaska and DiClemente model in 1983 when preparing to organize the Third International Conference on Treatment of Addictive Behaviours (ICTAB-3), which was eventually held at North Berwick in Scotland during August the following year. The idea for organizing this conference around the theme of the four stages of change – with separate components for Pre-contemplation, Contemplation, Action and Maintenance – came from the originator of the ICTAB series of conferences, William R. Miller of the University of New Mexico.

Although agreeing to the idea, I remember being a little sceptical about it; the attempt to force the contents of the invited addresses and, later on, the chapters of the book that emerged from the conference into the stages of change framework seemed somewhat procrustean; more fundamentally, I doubted whether the model added anything substantial to our understanding of change in the addictive behaviours. From the present perspective, these reservations seem akin to those of the man who doubted whether the Beatles would ever catch on!

Since the North Berwick conference, the stages of change model has become rapidly influential in the UK and several well-known treatment services are now based on it. Moreover, it is hardly possible to read an article on interventions for alcohol problems by a British author, particularly in relation to early intervention, without finding the model referred to.

It is still possible, of course, to be critical of the model. One wonders whether the process of change is quite so smooth and unidirectional as it seems to suggest, or whether change is often more fluctuating and inconsistent. Simply locating someone in one of the stages may not be enough to decide what type of intervention might be most appropriate; for example, within the Contemplation stage, there may be 'early' and 'late' contemplators who might need different types of motivational input. This clearly implies the need for further refinement of the model by research. More work is needed too on the basic problem of measuring readiness for change and reliably allocating people to the discrete stages of the model.

Nevertheless, it is as a simple but elegant heuristic device to assist thinking about a range of possible interventions, and how they can be matched to important characteristics of the problem drinker, that the model has proved most helpful. It has served the invaluable function of loosening thinking in this particular respect. Perhaps one of its most useful roles is in the continuing education of non-specialists, such as general practitioners and hospital doctors, who are given a logical framework for adjusting the advice they offer the excessive drinker to the individual's needs. As discussed in Chapter 1, it is also apparent that the model has a kind of face validity for many workers in the alcohol field and this presumably means that it is a meaningful enough representation of the manner in which change actually occurs in the real world. The model may have limited explanatory value, but its descriptive value is high.

I can also say that the stages of change model is becoming increasingly popular in Australia, although Bill Miller confirms that it has had far less effect, paradoxically, in the USA. It is interesting to speculate why this should be so. Perhaps we may risk a degree of complacency by concluding that there is an encouraging openness to new ideas and practices in the alcohol field in the UK and Australia at present. Certainly this splendid book would seem to support this conclusion.

Preface

The background to the New Directions in the Study of Alcohol Group

Gillian Tober

The study and treatment of alcohol problems was never a very popular subject. Uncertainty about whether the excessive use of alcohol was just bad behaviour or an intractable disease state was arguably even less attractive a proposition than whether in fact it was one or the other. Medical staff generally took the view that bad behaviour was not within their remit; probation officers took the view that intractable diseases were not within theirs. For psychologists a behaviour that could hardly be modified held little exploratory promise.

Just as the disease concept of alcoholism was being heralded as an advance in the state of the art, and one that could improve the lot of its sufferers by converting public and professional attitudes from negative sanction to constructive sympathy, evidence began to emerge which suggested yet another explanatory framework.

In 1962 D.L. Davies published a follow-up study of ninety-three former alcohol addicts, seven of whom had resumed normal drinking (Davies 1962). This report seriously questioned the basis of the disease concept of alcoholism, namely that the condition implied lifelong loss of control over the use of alcohol. It is unlikely that many follow-up studies have been met with the excited reaction enjoyed by Dr Davies, and the publishing journal subsequently carried an impressive quantity of varyingly fierce reactions to the findings. The naive bystander would have been forgiven for being surprised by the extreme reactions to such modest research findings. However, a number of intrepid explorers in the field of human behaviour took up the challenge laid down by these outcome data and set about attempting to improve upon the 'naturally occurring' phenomenon of resumed normal use, by giving alcohol to alcoholics in an experimental situation and teaching them to control their intake. In 1975 Lovibond presented a report of one such study in Sydney, Australia. A year later the findings of these successful controlled drinking trials were published and similar work was conducted elsewhere (Caddy and Lovibond 1976).

A new theoretical paradigm was required to explain the observed phenomena and to guide the experimental conditions in which they might be replicated. Social learning theory emerged as the framework most adequate to explain the interaction of biological, social and psychological factors in the aetiology and outcome of problem drinking. The sheer wealth of possible interventions, both preventive and remedial, implied an invitation to a multitude of professional groups from medicine, biochemistry and pharmacology through social, youth and community work to law, education and psychology to make a contribution to research and practice in the alcohol problems field. The isolation experienced by members of the different groups from colleagues within their professions could be compensated by the emergence of a supportive peer group in the multidisciplinary alcohol studies specialism.

The enthusiasm generated by this opening up of the alcohol field to new possibilities in research and practice required a forum – for debate, encouragement, and mutual support in the initiation of new research, new treatments and new services.

In 1976 a group of nurses, doctors, social workers and psychologists met at the Crichton Royal Hospital in Dumfries to discuss their mutual interest in resumed normal drinking as an outcome of therapy with alcoholics. It was proposed that the group be kept in being, and a clearing house for information and agreed terminology to facilitate research was also agreed. The meeting was followed by three more during the late 1970s, culminating in the inauguration of the New Directions in the Study of Alcohol Group (NDSAG) in Southport in 1980.

A constitution was written, financial independence and political neutrality were declared; NDSAG described itself as a 'talking shop' whose purpose was to encourage its members, both old and new, vigorously to pursue the investigation and implementation of new interventions for problem drinkers. There was a feeling, implicit in the name of the group, that these would be endlessly forthcoming: such was the optimism generated in this new era in the alcohol field.

Membership grew as new people came into the field and sought a peer group where informal discussion and presentation of ideas and work in embryo was encouraged. Discoveries made in the 1960s and 1970s continue to stimulate debate in the wider arena, though in the UK and much of Europe the controlled drinking controversy is abated. The 'new directions' in research and practice do not constitute a radical departure so much as a process of continually refining and developing our methods. The need to share difficulties and achievements from 'work in progress' continues to provide the impetus for like-minded professionals to meet, debate and describe their work in annual meetings, in bi-annual booklets and in this, the second New Directions in the Study of Alcohol book.

References

Caddy, G.R. and Lovibond, S.H. (1976) 'Self-regulation and discriminated aversive conditioning in the modification of alcoholics' drinking behaviour', *Behaviour Therapy* 7: 223–30.
Davies, D.L. (1962) 'Normal drinking in recovered alcohol addicts', *Quarterly Journal of Studies on Alcohol* 23: 94–104.

Part one

The process of change

Chapter one

Facilitating change in problem drinkers

Robin Davidson

Many people spend much of their working lives trying to help others resolve a drinking problem. The helpers are usually diligent and caring but sometimes frustrated. They are faced with a behaviour which is characterized, perhaps more than anything else, by its unpredictability and propensity for change. If the helpers have read a few books on the treatment of drinking problems their frustration may be compounded. Numerous therapies are touted by their proponents while independent reviewers are often equivocal and conclude that the outcome for problem drinkers is strikingly similar, no matter which treatment is used. How do conscientious helpers choose a strategy of intervention which will be best for their clients? How can helpers match the most appropriate intervention to the current needs of the clients?

This book is not a review of the efficacy of various treatments but rather is an attempt to provide therapists and counsellors with a framework, based on a process of change, to assist with their case-management decisions. In the first part of the book interventions are discussed and placed in context, with the emphasis being on practice rather than theory. The second part is an attempt to relate the process of change model to more general service delivery issues. By way of introduction it may be useful to examine the nature of treatment and change as applied to problem drinking.

The nature of treatment

'Treatment' is an unfortunate word and remains part of our legacy from the days when alcoholism was regarded, in an almost literal sense, as a disease. It is now clear that the sophistry of the disease view cannot come close to accounting adequately for the complexity of factors which contribute to the development of an individual's drinking problem.

The word 'treatment' carries with it connotations of a palliative insertion into the life of a problem drinker administered by an external therapist to a passive patient. It promotes the view of patients in a sick role with no personal responsibility for their condition and implies that intervention is a short-term bridge from illness to cure.

If we are to use the word 'treatment' then it should perhaps be a shorthand for a *set of potentially long-term facilitative events which can help the individual readapt*. When used in this way it carries with it a number of issues which should be addressed.

1 It is better to place treatment in the context of a 'drinking career'. This is a psychosocial construct which takes account of the various environmental influences from birth to death which shape individuals' drinking behaviour and must be understood in terms of the culture in which they live. Treatment could then be seen as an ongoing interaction between therapeutic input and the unfolding career; indeed it should be matched to the stages of the evolving career. Treatment, when viewed in this way, is a series of strategies which hopefully will have the effect of edging an individual into a less destructive, long-term career path. Edwards (1989) puts it succinctly: 'Treatment', he argues, 'should be conceived of as being at best a timely nudge or whisper in a long life course'.

2 Treatment processes are not necessarily distinct from the so-called naturally occurring processes of change. The work of Prochaska and DiClemente (1984), summarized on pp. 12–17, demonstrates that so-called 'self-changers' can informally employ most of the strategies described in formal therapeutic systems. Indeed many problem drinkers who successfully deal with their problem do so without recourse to formal treatment (Saunders and Kershaw 1979).

3 A related issue is the intensity of treatment required when a person does opt for the treatment route. Since the seminal work of Orford and Edwards (1977) on 'Treatment versus Advice', there have been a substantial number of evaluative studies (e.g. Chapman and Huygens 1988) which have concluded that for many problem drinkers, particularly those who are less severely dependent, intensive prolonged treatment does not seem to have any significant long-term advantage over simpler, less intensive interventions. While it is not appropriate to summarize this body of work here there are a number of cautionary caveats which should be added to this finding. First, treatment intensity experiments are difficult to do properly. Orford (1980), for

example, concedes that even the Treatment versus Advice study was by no means methodologically flawless. Second, in few of the major studies to date has there been an attempt to match the client with the therapy in any systematic way. Third, and arguably most important, when intensity and cost are taken together, Room (1980) reminds us that the basic justification of providing treatment should be primarily for reasons of humanity rather than cost-benefit analysis.

4 It may be that so-called 'non-specific' aspects of the treatment process can be instrumental in facilitating change. It is not immediately apparent from the literature that long-term changes necessarily occur for the reasons we think they do. For example Russell *et al.* (1976) found that a technically incorrect behavioural programme was just as effective as one which was correctly implemented. It would of course be quite wrong to abandon treatments which have been generated from a sound theoretical base. Social learning theory is particularly useful in this regard. It is none the less wise to remember that individuals are potential changers from the moment they present. Initial interview, assessment, therapy, follow-up and rehabilitation can all be part of the process of change.

5 Whatever the type or style of treatment, both therapist and client bring personal characteristics to the therapeutic dialogue which can significantly influence outcome. Clearly therapists differ in terms of personality, training, orientation and experience. Indeed, in the treatment of general psychological disorder Murphy *et al.* (1984) found that most clients tended to attribute the effectiveness of treatment to empathy and understanding on the part of the therapist while most therapists, not unnaturally, attributed success to their particular technique.

Client characteristics also affect outcome. In an important study Costello (1980) demonstrated that social stability had a powerful and direct link with outcome. Other client characteristics which can influence outcome have been listed by Rix and Rix (1983) and include socioeconomic status, age, length of drinking history and degree of dependence. It is important to appreciate, however, that these indicators may work in different directions according to how treatment and outcome are defined. In one of the most extensive follow-up studies ever conducted, Armor (1980) found that older, highly dependent men were less likely to have relapsed after four years if they were abstainers rather than controlled drinkers eighteen months after treatment. For younger, less dependent men the reverse seemed to be true. For older men of medium dependence and for young men of high dependence marital status was also an important predictor of successful outcome.

6 Next is the once vexed issue of treatment goal. The idea of a controlled or harm-free drinking goal symbolizes perhaps more than anything the difference between traditional and more recent approaches to the management of drinking problems. For this reason the debate has been conducted at a more personal and anecdotal level than is normally the case in scientific discourse. In their studious and thorough review of the literature Heather and Robertson (1985) leave the open-minded reader in no doubt that a drinking goal should be considered when the therapist and client are formulating their treatment strategy. The question should not be 'Can some alcoholics drink normally?' as the literature is replete with examples to show that they can. Rather we should be asking which clients will benefit most from abstinence and who should be aiming for controlled drinking. There is an urgent need for further systematic evaluation of indicators like degree of dependence, attribution style, beliefs and expectations which will assist the therapist and client make an educated choice about the optimum treatment goal.

7 Finally, the question has been asked many times: 'Does treatment work?' Reviewers have arrived at various conclusions. Some are negative like Schachter (1982), who argues that the quality of recovery is better in spontaneous changers than those who have been through treatment. Some like Saunders (1985) are neutral. He concluded his review rather graphically: 'the treatment emperor is naked and pretending all is well only delays the advent of new and better responses'. Some argue that a specific approach, like that based on social learning theory, holds much promise (Rollnick 1985). Most reviewers, however, would be guardedly positive and would agree with Raistrick and Davidson (1985), who conclude that treatment can improve outcome although no particular treatment approach has emerged as being consistently superior to the others.

This is a brief and by no means exhaustive list of some of the issues involved in the contribution of treatment to the process of change. It is not meant to leave the reader with a sense of what is commonly called in the alcohol literature 'therapeutic nihilism', but rather, it is an attempt to provide a backdrop against which to consider the treatment strategies discussed in succeeding chapters.

The process of change

One of the doyens of British psychology, George Kelly (1969), has argued that movement is an essential property of humankind's being. Indeed he said that life itself could be defined as a 'form of process or movement'. All of us make decisions and, perhaps as a result, alter our behaviour, attitudes and cognitions over time. This could encompass a whole range of human activity, for example our prejudices, political beliefs, self-perceptions, as well as eating and drinking habits.

Social psychologists are becoming increasingly interested in the prerequisites and nature of decision-making and change. Pentony (1981) suggests there is a consensus in the psychotherapy literature that the process of change and relearning new procedures involves at least three stages. There is an initial destructuring when old behaviours are attenuated, an intermediate period of confusion and a final stage of restructuring. Ryle (1984) argues that different therapies vary in the emphasis which they place on each of these stages. In their book, *Decision Making: A Psychological Analysis of Conflict, Choice and Commitment*, Janis and Mann (1977) analyse how all sorts of life decisions are made and, more importantly, carried through. Central to their model is the idea that psychological change is precipitated by conflict and perceived loss. What is apposite to the present discussion is their view that the general process of decision-making and change proceeds through a number of stages, namely reappraisal, considering the options, selection, action and consolidation. They also say that fully consolidated change takes time and that reversion to earlier stages of the process can sometimes occur.

The work of Janis and Mann underlies the ideas of Orford (1985), whose scholarly and authoritative book *Excessive Appetites* provides us with a general theoretical synthesis of the psychology of addiction without recourse to the notion of a disease. Before considering models of change within addictions, however, it may help our understanding to outline briefly two specific examples of the change drawn from other areas of human activity.

Specific examples of change

In the early 1970s Cross and his colleagues (Cross 1971; Hall *et al.* 1972) examined the way individual black Americans developed a racial identity. They argued that black people progress through a series of well-defined stages, as they gradually encounter blackness in themselves. In what they called the 'Negro to Black conversion experience' people can develop from a point when they may be uncomfortable with their colour to a completely secure racial identity. The four stages of this process are described as pre-encounter, encounter, immersion–emmersion and internalization. In the first stage individuals view the world as being non- or anti-black and can behave in ways which devalue their black identity, while during the second stage they gradually become aware of what it means to be black. This encounter stage of self-examination is characterized by transition and confusion. In the third stage individuals tend to reject white values and immerse themselves almost exclusively in black culture. In the final stage, internalization, individuals develop a self-confident and secure black identity but can also feel comfortable with the mores and prejudices of people from other cultures. Within each stage there is a complex interaction of behaviours, attitudes, emotions and cognitions although the model tends to concentrate on the process of attitudinal change. What is particularly interesting is that Cross and his colleagues began by postulating five stages. However, after a series of factor-analytic validation studies they found that a four-stage model better described the data. This is very similar to the evolution of the model proposed by Prochaska and DiClemente (1984). The elements of the Negro to Black conversion experience have been operationalized in the Racial Identity Scale thoroughly validated by Ponterotto and Wise (1987). This work highlights that attitudinal change can evolve through a series of stages which can be empirically identified.

Another more anecdotal example of change will be familiar to readers who live in the southern regions of the USA, Scotland and Northern Ireland. In these cultures there is a strong fundamentalist religious tradition in which the emphasis is on religious conversion and subsequent commitment to a new more spiritual life-style. At the risk of caricature, what is said to occur is that such conversion can produce substantial cognitive and behavioural change which impacts on many areas of individuals' day-to-day lives and which for some can be maintained indefinitely without recourse to their erstwhile life-style. In discussion with a considerable number of advocates of 'old-style religion' I have been struck by their understanding of the process of change involved in religious conversion. They argue that many people are not interested in changing their behaviour or beliefs. Some, however, have moved to a stage in which they are unhappy with their current life-style and who report much introspection, doubt and confusion. They experience inconsistencies in their attitudes towards themselves or others, which social psychologists would call cognitive dissonance and fundamentalist theologians would describe as a period when the 'spirit is striving'. After a time these individuals make a commitment to change, or as it is termed 'conversion', which is followed by a period of vigilance during which integration of the new beliefs is said to occur in the context of increasingly altered behaviour. Inevitably some people relapse, or in fundamentalist parlance, 'backslide'. Here again we see a graded process which is characterized not by its suddenness but rather by its development over time.

As an aside, this is of course not the first time that religious ideas have been used as a metaphor to assist understanding of practice in the alcohol field. We know that Alcoholics Anonymous (AA) was significantly influenced by the Oxford group, a religious organization in the evangelical protestant tradition. The central features of Oxford practice were group identity, open confession and sharing with other members. Bill W. (1957) acknowledged the importance of the Oxford group in the development of AA ideas on self-examination admitting to character deficits and restitution. The principles of change espoused by religious groups have maybe been regarded with some scepticism by behavioural scientists, who have viewed addictions from a much more empirical perspective. Equally, work on the therapist characteristics which facilitate change has not really taken account of variables regarded as important by religious groups such as the charisma and power of the therapist. Other methods used to promote change by such groups for example symbolism, open sharing and pledge-taking have also been studied less rigorously than perhaps they should. Orford (1986) reminds us that when 'modern' treatments of alcohol dependence are examined closely they are a subtle blend of the spiritual and the scientific. While we should not, of course, return to the moral persuasion techniques of these people, there is an argument that strategies which seem to promote psychological change in other areas should not be summarily dismissed, just because they fail to fit comfortably with our own views of addictive behaviour.

Returning to the main theme of the discussion, the work summarized in this section demonstrates that any model of behavioural or attitudinal change should enable us to chart the stages inherent in the decision-making process as well as the critical conditions which facilitate or impede change.

Models of change in addiction

The idea that the route into and out of an addiction is characterized by psychological changes which can to some extent be operationalized and identified is nothing new. Most of us who see problem drinkers notice that some redefine their relationship with alcohol and alter their behaviour accordingly as time goes by.

In what is arguably the most famous alcohol artefact of all, Glatt's U-shaped curve, various stages in the development of alcohol dependence and recovery are charted (Glatt 1972). Heather and Robertson (1985) quite rightly point out that the underlying assumptions of this model are flawed in that they have more to do with nineteenth-century moral warnings against the dangers of alcohol than a clear conception of the psychosocial nature of a drug using 'career'. It does none the less represent an early attempt to define some of the behavioural and attitudinal phases of the journey into and out of alcohol dependence.

It is becoming clear, however, that there are commonalties in the process of decision-making and change which apply not just to alcohol dependence, but to a whole range of human activity. Rarely, for example, do smokers report the moral deterioration or vague spiritual desires annotated in Glatt's model of alcoholism. A comprehensive model of change in addiction should advance our understanding of how people alter behaviours like smoking, drug use, gambling and over-eating. Equally such a model should account for improvement which is not necessarily induced by formal methods of treatment. As suggested above, so-called spontaneous remission is not an instantaneous mysterious recovery but is similar in nature to therapeutically induced change. It is a useful starting-point, therefore, when formulating ideas on the process of change, to take account of the opinions of successful self-changers.

Tuchfeld (1976) did just this by carefully interviewing over fifty problem drinkers who had successfully recovered without presenting themselves to any treatment agency. On the basis of these interviews he proposed what is essentially a two-stage model of change. As the perceived losses in the drinker's balance sheet outweigh the gains the individual moves to a stage when defensive avoidance becomes untenable and a commitment to change is made. The conflict which precedes this may occur as a gradual build up or alternatively may happen quite suddenly. After making a commitment, Tuchfeld argues that it is followed by the maintenance stage of personal vigilance, during which time the individual develops coping strategies to attenuate the possibility of relapse. A commitment to change is all very well but it should subsequently be supported by hard work on the development of maintenance factors. The traditional six-week in-patient treatment programmes for alcoholics using confrontational group therapy may have emphasized commitment at the expense of the maintenance. Indeed it has been demonstrated that successful outcome can be more related to post-treatment than treatment factors (Billings and Moos 1983).

The work of Tuchfeld demonstrates the need for good and detailed data gleaned from relatively unstructured interviews to give the reader a flavour of the huge range of events, conditions and self-perceptions which can promote change. This approach is used in Chapter 8 and is a salutory reminder that treatment is not an end in itself. At best it interacts with past developmental events and its effect is filtered by those of the future.

Because of the limitations of purely behavioural treatment methods psychologists have moved towards the view that people shape their environment as much as they are influenced by it. Individuals can actively organize their external and internal environment to influence the possibility of certain behaviours occurring. This has given rise to the self-control or self-regulation approach to the management of drinking problems. Arising from this perspective, Kanfer and Grimm (1980) have proposed a model which details stages of change and helps therapists match their activities to the needs of clients as they progress through therapy. The strength of the model is that it is firmly based on the principles of self-regulation. Although the latter have been criticized as being a collection of observations rather than a comprehensive theory, they do emphasize the interaction between people and their environment and generate new approaches to treatment which are testable and open to disconfirmation.

Kanfer and Grimm (1980) have suggested that there are a number of critical transition points as individuals define themselves as in need of change and then attempt to act on this redefinition. Kanfer and Grimm suggest a number of pre-therapy phases. Individuals become aware of the problems and then consciously evaluate their impact on their life. If individuals make a decision to seek help they are encouraged in the preparatory phase to assume responsibility, define their problems more explicitly and focus on the conditions which will facilitate change. In these first stages the overall therapeutic goal is to 'motivate the client towards a commitment for change' (Kanfer 1986). It is argued that the phases which precede explicit behavioural change are rarely discussed in treatment manuals but are just as important as the choice of techniques used to develop and strengthen new behaviour. In the action stage clients actively alter their daily living activities to minimize the risk of relapse. The emphasis here is on anticipating future situations and preparing appropriate coping strategies. The final stage is one of evaluation. Clients should be confident that they have the necessary skills which are sufficiently generalized thus enabling them to deal with unforeseen future difficulties. Furthermore they should have planned more substantial life changes to provide an environment incompatible with their previous addictive behaviour. Specific self-control methods of intervention which are appropriate in the preparatory, action and evaluative stages will be presented in more detail in later chapters.

The integrative model of change

The most recent and arguably most influential model of change is the integrative model first proposed by Prochaska and DiClemente in 1983. It is their model which has been used to organize and present the material in this book. It has stimulated much debate and has provided a framework which has helped workers organize their knowledge and make case-management decisions.

Later Prochaska and DiClemente (1984) argued that an integrative model of change should have the following properties, some of which have been highlighted above.

1 It should account for the behaviour of self-changers as well as those who have been through therapy.
2 It should be applicable to a wide range of addictive behaviour.
3 It should help workers synthesize the various treatment methods currently available.
4 It should cover the course of change from the time someone begins to acknowledge the problem to the point when it appears to be fully resolved.

What they called their transtheoretical approach is based on a three-dimensional model which was originally validated on a large cohort of successful ex-smokers. The three dimensions are the stages, processes and levels of change.

The stages of change
The authors suggest that people are at various stages in their willingness to change which are not dissimilar to the stages in some of the models discussed in the previous section. Successful change generally involves progressing from pre-contemplation to contemplation to action and then to maintenance.

Within **pre-contemplation** individuals are not aware of their difficulties, perhaps as a result of ambivalence, denial or selective exposure to information. As individuals become aware that their alcohol or drug use constitutes a problem they are said to have entered the **contemplation** stage. The individual is admitting that something is wrong and is seriously thinking about change. This can last for months, even years, and indeed some people never go beyond contemplation. The **action** stage is much shorter, yet paradoxically is where most overt progress is made. When I was discussing the model with Don Bannister, before his untimely death, he made the pertinent comment that the action stage is analogous to the age-old idea of reaching a turning-point in life when a commitment to alter behaviour is made. Once making the decision to change, the individual enters the **maintenance** stage in which the new habits are strengthened. This continues until self-efficacy or the feeling that one is now in control of the addiction is maximized. The individual then exits the change system to termination, that is, favourable long-term outcome.

For many who are attempting to alter addictive behaviour, **relapse** is common, notably in the first six months or so. After the vigilance of maintaining the new behaviour for a time, the determinants of relapse can include negative self-evaluation, environmental pressures or inadequately prepared coping styles (Marlatt and George 1984). Whatever the cause, the relapser can either exit back to pre-contemplation and give up trying or alternatively re-enter the change process. Thus individuals do not progress in a linear fashion but rather in the more cyclical pattern presented in Figure 1.1. It is said, for example, that on average, successful ex-smokers make three serious revolutions through the stages of change before becoming free of the habit.

As was the case with the racial identity model of Cross (1971) outlined above, Prochaska and DiClemente originally proposed five stages but multivariate analysis of a set of test items produced only four distinct factors.

The processes of change

It is suggested that there are a number of processes of change which can modify emotions, behaviour or cognitions. Prochaska and DiClemente based this idea on an analysis of the intervention strategies used in a wide range of therapeutic systems. Ten common central processes were isolated.

Each process is basically a category of treatment activities all of which have something in common. This is despite the fact that the therapeutic systems from which the categories were drawn have different underlying theoretical assumptions about the aetiology and treatment of psychopathology. An example may help clarify this. One category of activity is consciousness-raising, which Prochaska and DiClemente argue is part of many diverse therapy

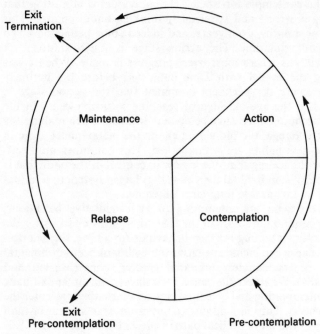

Figure 1.1 Stages of individual change
Source: Adapted from Prochaska and DiClemente 1984

systems. Techniques for increasing consciousness could include the didactic approaches of the educationalist, the confrontational techniques of the rational emotive therapist, the observational and video-feedback techniques of the behaviour therapist and the interpretatons of the psychoanalyist. What all these therapeutic strategies have in common is their putative usefulness in helping clients become more aware of themselves and their problems. The set of ten change processes or categories of activity are presented in Table 1.1. As pointed out by Ryle (1984) most systems of therapy will of course only emphasize two or three of these and will differ in terms of whether they are applied experientially or environment-ally. However, data from successful self-changers suggest that they employ strategies from almost all of the categories. The authors therefore urge therapists to adopt an eclectic approach in that they should be prepared to intervene with a comprehensive set of change activities when necessary.

Table 1.1 The catalysts of change

1	Consciousness-raising
2	Self-re-evaluation
3	Environmental re-evaluation
4	Self-liberation
5	Social-liberation
6	Counter-conditioning
7	Stimulus control
8	Contingency management
9	Dramatic relief
10	Helping relationships

Integration of stage and process

There is said to be an interaction between stage and process, that is particular therapeutic interventions are more appropriate for each stage. Prochaska and DiClemente (1984) suggest, for example, that verbal strategies which emphasize consciousness-raising are most effective during the contemplation stage. Alternatively behavioural techniques, for example stimulus control or contingency management, may be more appropriate in the maintenance stage. Cognitive approaches which take account of abstinence violation effects and attempt to improve self-efficacy or self-esteem may be most useful for people who have just relapsed.

Therapy must, however, be seen against the backdrop of unfolding life events which are taking place outside the treatment agency. The effect of relationships, promotion, redundancy, ageing, accidents, illnesses, births or deaths can stultify, neutralize or facilitate the counsellor's endeavour. It would seem that progress, particularly from pre-contemplation to contemplation, is primarily due to developmental or environmental changes. Prochaska and DiClemente (1983) suggest for example that the age of 40 is a key developmental point for re-evaluation. Of the cohort of successful ex-smokers, people began to contemplate change at a mean age of 39. The authors acidly observe that 39 is indeed a mean age.

Other people can begin contemplation because of events in their external environment and therapists should take account of such influences as they formulate a treatment programme. The work of Vaillant (1982) is a salutory reminder to all of us in the change business that we retain humility and view our treatment within a longitudinal perspective. The influence of life events on the process of change is the subject of Chapter 8.

Levels of change

It is axiomatic to say that creating and maintaining change in any human activity is not simple and can occur at a number of different levels. Each of these levels of psychological functioning can be addressed in treatment. The simplest is that of the presenting symptoms for which operant or behavioural strategies are the most effective. The next is the level of cognition or maladaptive thought patterns. Cognitive therapists would normally work at this level in that they are primarily dealing with the individual's beliefs and expectations which can profoundly influence behaviour. The third level is interpersonal conflicts, then family/system conflict and finally deeper intrapersonal conflict. This last level is usually thought to be primarily the domain of the psychoanalyst. Prochaska and DiClemente suggest it is critical that therapists are alert as to which level they attribute the problem and accordingly at which level or levels they are willing to work with each individual client.

The general integrative model of change has been summarized briefly and perhaps over-simplified in translation. It can be seen, however, that the model emphasizes integration across a range of treatment interventions as well as the essential heterogeneity of our client group.

Assessment of the stages of change

Therapists who use this model as a guide to the most appropriate treatment approach often make a judgement about the stages of change based on their knowledge of the characteristics of each stage. Prochaska and DiClemente have produced the Stages of Change questionnaire consisting of thirty-two self-statements, which are said to assess the four key stages in a highly reliable and statistically powerful manner. This test was developed largely for research purposes and is certainly useful as a screening implement for fairly heterogeneous samples but where groups of people are self-selected, for example those presenting at a treatment agency, it seems to discriminate less well between the four stages. A similar but shorter test is currently being developed in the UK and shows some promise (Rollnick 1990), although its psychometric properties have still to be fully investigated.

Critique of the integrative model of change

Prochaska and DiClemente's integrative model of change is now recognized as being useful for ordering our knowledge and providing guidance on how best to intervene with alcohol-dependent clients. It has gained wide acceptance for a number of reasons. First, its emphasis on eclecticism probably appeals to those therapists who have become disillusioned with the reductionism of behaviour therapy or the intuitive, hermeneutic approach of psychotherapy. Second, while it is not simple, the model is comprehensible to the counsellor faced with day-to-day issues involved in edging people out of a drinking problem. Third, the model is clearly applicable to a variety of addictive behaviours which people may wish to change.

Like everything else the integrative model of change is not without its critics and it would be a prejudicial account which did not acknowledge some of its short-comings.

1 Although it is comprehensible the integrative model may be too comprehensive. There are some problems with molar, expansive models which seek to describe all substance misuse. There are different levels of reality, for example biochemical, physiological, individual, social context and primary group relations. Consolidation of these levels is difficult as each has its own units of analysis and methods of enquiry. Warr (1980) points out that the clear initial structure of a model can become lost through the repeated addition of unconnected refinements so that it eventually loses the cohesion of purposeful configuration.

2 Addiction models can be evaluated like any other, for example the clearness and explicitness of rules, simplicity, the ability to define terms empirically, the possibility of submitting the model to the test of falsification, and the ability to suggest new relations and hypotheses. The reader is left to decide how the model fares against these criteria.

3 The authors describe the model as transtheoretical. A more apt description may be atheoretical. It is not intended to further our understanding of the nature, aetiology and development of addictive behaviour. At best the stages and processes of change provide us with navigation aids for a section of the individual's drinking career.

4 More specifically it is clear that not everyone who successfully deals with an addiction progresses in an orderly way through the aforementioned stages. Some do seem to be 'overnight successes'. Furthermore, Orford (1986) points out that, for others, change may occur because the behaviour in question loses its meaning or functional significance without individuals becoming consciously aware that they were changing at all.

Summary and vocabulary

Despite the criticisms, Prochaska and DiClemente's (1984) integrative model of change has had a significant impact on the delivery of care and has helped provide a synthesis of different treatment activities. As noted above this book is based on the model and has been written for people of all disciplines who are trying to promote change among alcohol-dependent clients. In the first section, each chapter explores a particular stage of change. There is a description of the stage, a number of illustrative case studies and a summary of the therapeutic interventions which could usefully be applied. Clearly some strategies may be beneficial for a range of clients. Equally some individuals may demonstrate features of a number of stages and not easily be located into one or the other. However, as far as possible each chapter attempts to describe the most relevant treatments, with overlap, although inevitable, being kept to a minimum. The chapters in Part One are not intended to be prescriptive. Counsellors should adapt the treatment suggestions to fit in with their client group, experience, work setting and therapeutic orientation.

In Part Two it is recognized that one-to-one counselling must of necessity take place within a personal, social, environmental and political context. Chapters 6, 7, 8 and 9 illustrate how the process of change model can assist understanding of issues beyond one-to-one counselling. These include running problem-solving groups, interpreting and predicting the effect of life events, adapting services to particular settings and planning a community service. This last chapter should be of interest to managers who may be responsible for the most effective deployment of resources.

Finally, as there is no common vocabulary, the editors have made a number of decisions on the terminology used in the book in order to preserve continuity of style. Those receiving help have been called 'clients'. This is seen as preferable to more loaded terms such as 'patient' or 'customer'. Helpers are referred to throughout as 'counsellors', although it would be equally valid to have used the word 'therapist' in this regard.

References

Armor, D.J. (1980) 'The Rand Reporting and the analysis of relapse', in G. Edwards and M. Grant (eds) *Alcoholism Treatment in Transition*, London: Croom Helm.

Bill W. (1957) *Alcoholics Anonymous Comes of Age: A Brief History of AA*, New York: Alcoholics Anonymous World Services.

Billings, A. and Moos, R. (1983) 'Psychosocial processes of recovery among alcoholics and their families: implications for clinicians and programme evaluators', *Addictive Behaviours* 8: 205–18.

Chapman, P.L. and Huygens, I. (1988) 'An evaluation of three treatment programs for alcoholism: an experimental study with 6 and 18 months follow-ups', *British Journal of Addiction* 83: 67–81.

Costello, R.M. (1980) 'Alcoholism treatment effectiveness: slicing the outcome variance pie', in G. Edwards and M. Grant (eds) *Alcoholism Treatment in Transition*, London: Croom Helm.

Cross, W.E. (1971) 'The Negro to black conversion experience: toward a psychology of black liberation', *Black World* 20: 13–27.

Edwards, G. (1989) 'As the years go rolling by: drinking problems in the time dimension', *British Journal of Psychiatry* 154: 18–26.

Glatt, M.M. (1972) *The Alcoholic and the Help He Needs*, London: Priory Press.

Hall, W., Cross, W. and Freedle, R. (1972) 'Stages in the development of black awareness: an exploratory investigation', in R. Jones (ed.) *Black Psychology*, New York: Harper & Row.

Heather, N. and Robertson, I. (1985) *Controlled Drinking*, 2nd edn, New York: Methuen.

Janis, I. and Mann, L. (1977) *Decision Making: A Psychological Analysis of Conflict, Choice and Commitment*, New York: Free Press.

Kanfer, F.H. (1986) 'Implications of a self-regulation model of therapy for treatment of addictive behaviours', in W.R. Miller and N. Heather (eds) *Treating Addictive Behaviours: Process of Change*, New York: Plenum Press.

Kanfer, F.H. and Grimm G.L. (1980) 'Managing clinical change: a process model of therapy', *Behaviour Modification* 4: 419–44.

Kelly, G. (1969) 'The psychotherapeutic relationship', in B. Maher (ed.) *Clinical Psychology and Personality*, New York: Krieger.

Marlatt, A.G. and George, W.H. (1984) 'Relapse preventions: introduction and overview of the model', *British Journal of Addiction* 79: 261–74.

Murphy, P.M., Cramer, D. and Lillie, F.J. (1984) 'The relationship between curative factors perceived by patients in their psychotherapy and treatment outcome: an exploratory study', *British Journal of Medical Psychology* 57: 187–92.

Orford, J. (1980) 'Understanding treatment: controlled trials and other strategies', in G. Edwards and M. Grant (eds) *Alcoholism Treatment in Transition*, London: Croom Helm.

—— (1985) *Excessive Appetites: A Psychological View of Addictions*, Chichester, John Wiley.

—— (1986) 'Critical conditions for change in the addictive behaviours', in W.R. Miller and N. Heather (eds) *Treating Addictive Behaviours: Process of Change*, New York: Plenum Press.

Orford, J. and Edwards, G. (1977) 'Alcoholism: a comparison of treatment and advice with a study of the influence of marriage', *Maudsley Monograph No 26*, Oxford: Oxford University Press.

Pentony, P. (ed.) (1981) *Models of Influence in Psychotherapy*, New York: Free Press.

Ponterotto, J. and Wise, S. (1987) 'Construct validity study of the

19

Racial Identity Attitude Scale', *Journal of Counselling Psychology* 14: 218–23.

Prochaska, J.O. and DiClemente, C.C. (1983) 'Stages and processes of self-change of smoking: toward an integrated model of change', *Journal of Consulting Clinical Psychology* 51: 390–5.

—— (1984) *The Transtheoretical Approach: Crossing Traditional Boundaries of Therapy*, New York: Daw-Jones Irwin.

Raistrick, D. and Davidson, R. (1985) *Alcoholism and Drug Addiction*, London: Churchill Livingstone.

Rix, J.B. and Rix, E.L. (1983) *Alcohol Problems: A Guide for Nurses and Other Health Professionals*, Bristol: Wright.

Rollnick, S. (1985) 'The value of a cognitive-behavioural approach in the treatment of problem drinkers', in N. Heather, I. Robertson and P. Davies (eds) *The Misuse of Alcohol: Crucial Issues in Dependence Treatment and Prevention*, London: Croom Helm.

—— (1990) Personal communication.

Room, R. (1980) 'New curves in the course: a comment on Polich, Armor, and Braiker, *The Course of Alcoholism*', *British Journal of Addiction* 5: 351–60.

Russell, M., Armstrong, E. and Patel, U. (1976) 'Temporal continuity in electric aversion therapy for cigarette smoking', *Behaviour Research and Therapy* 14: 103–23.

Ryle, A. (1984) 'How can we compare different psychotherapies? Why are they effective?' *British Journal of Medical Psychology* 57: 261–4.

Saunders, B. (1985) 'Treatment does not work: some criteria of failure', in N. Heather, I. Robertson and P. Davies (eds) *The Misuses of Alcohol: Crucial Issues in Dependence, Treatment and Prevention*, London: Croom Helm.

Saunders, W.M. and Kershaw, P.W. (1979) 'Spontaneous remission from alcoholism: a community study', *British Journal of Addiction* 74: 251–65.

Schachter, S. (1982) 'Recidivism and self-care of smoking and obesity', *American Psychologist* 37, 4: 436–44.

Tuchfeld, B. (1976) 'Changes in the patterns of alcohol use without the aid of formal treatment', *Research Triangle Institute*, North Carolina.

Vaillant, C. (1982) *The Natural History of Alcoholism*, New York: Yale University Press.

Warr, S. (1980) 'An introduction to models in psychological research', in A.J. Chapman and D.M. Jones (eds) *Models of Man*, Leicester: British Psychological Society.

Chapter two

Helping the pre-contemplator

Gillian Tober

What is the pre-contemplation stage?

People in pre-contemplation have presented the alcohol problems field with its greatest challenge. They are the problem drinkers who 'do not want to be helped' and if they do approach agencies, they are often turned away with 'there's nothing we can do for you until you decide to give up drinking'. One fairly widespread view is that effective interventions are not available for this group; naturally occurring phenomena may change their minds about their drinking and only then will help be available. This chapter is an attempt to change this view.

People in pre-contemplation are those problem drinkers who say they don't have a problem with alcohol, or that they can't do anything about their drinking. For our present purpose, this group does not include people who never had, or no longer have, a problem with alcohol, or those who are in a state of passive ignorance about the harmful consequences of their drinking. Rather the focus of this chapter is that group of people who actively make and remake the decision to carry on drinking in spite of the harm it may be doing to themselves and other people.

When drinking fulfils very important needs, when the individual believes these needs cannot be fulfilled elsewhere, the drinking will come to be seen as the solution, not the problem. This sets the scene for conflict between the individual and others: family, friends, employers and alcohol counsellors. In fact it sets the scene for conflict *within* the individual. In order to be able to continue drinking the conflict must be resolved, and it will be resolved by underplaying the extent of the drinking, or by underplaying the problems it causes.

Case study   Being a pre-contemplator

For the past five years Stephanie has been drinking a lot – often up to a bottle of gin a day. Usually she conceals her drinking and claims her husband accuses her unjustly; after all, his shirts are ironed and the children are fed.

For the past thirteen years Stephanie has been a housewife and mother. Before that she worked with an advertising agency as a personal assistant and enjoyed the glamour and frequent entertaining. Her marriage put an abrupt end to her career because her husband, in the pursuit of his, was required to move – four times in four years. Stephanie got pregnant at the beginning of the marriage and continued to get pregnant at two-year intervals until she had three children. Four years later she had a fourth child. Each move had taken her further away from friends and family, each child tying her more and more to her home. She didn't complain; her mother had done it, her mother-in-law too. It was an unspoken agreement between herself and her husband that she would do it. Anyway, over the years she had discovered that a bottle of gin made the day go by in an agreeable manner; after all, that's what she'd done with her friends in the evenings and weekends before she'd had to move away.

In the past five years things had got difficult; her husband had started to insult her and once had even hit her. She felt awful on some mornings. She couldn't face the kids or the housework until she'd had another drink; neither could she have another drink until her husband had left for the office.

One day Stephanie's husband said 'You're an alcoholic and if you don't do something about your drinking I'll have you sent away'. She would not leave the children – not on any account. So she went to a clinic for detoxification. Two weeks later she felt much better and was glad of it. 'Now then, I had better be more careful in future, make sure he doesn't find out'.

Stephanie has no intention of changing her life-style; she wants to be a 'good wife and mother'. Alcohol might not be the perfect solution (she knows it is 'not good for her', she knows it makes her husband angry, she knows it makes her feel rotten the next morning), but it is a very handy solution for a lot of things.

After taking the children to school she can settle down with the paper and a gin and tonic while the baby is asleep, and before having to get the others home for lunch. The same in the afternoon. Then when her husband comes home from work, he seems more keen to play with the children when she has been drinking. If she's angry with him, a couple of drinks help her to say so, and if she has to go to one of those 'ghastly office dos' a couple of drinks certainly make her feel less anxious, less boring. On balance it may be a bit worrying, but a gulp of booze does help on very difficult mornings.

In this case study, Stephanie sees her drinking as the best, possibly the only solution to the difficulties in her life. Therefore the benefits of drinking *outweigh* the costs. It is not the case that she perceives no problems, but rather that she diminishes the importance of the problems. Feeling sweaty and shaky in the morning is not so bad as being bored all day, or nervously anticipating office parties. Having something readily to hand to calm her down is far more important than the vague threat of her marriage breaking down or her liver being damaged. Rationalizations like 'my husband would never leave me' and 'my smoking will kill me before my drinking does' are used to get rid of any conflicting thoughts the drinking might be causing.

Therapeutic interventions

The variety of goals for work in pre-contemplation is described in this section, and methods of intervention designed to meet one set of goals, namely damage limitation, are described in detail on pp. 27–38.

Ensuring contact with pre-contemplators

One reason for the fact that people in pre-contemplation are least likely to be seen in specialist agencies is the negative reaction with which they have traditionally been met. People who 'deny their drinking', who are 'not motivated to change', have been sent away until they have changed their mind about their drinking. More enlightened agencies have failed to engage them by virtue of the absence of interventions appropriate to this group.

Clearly the possibility of offering any intervention depends upon establishing and maintaining contact with the problem drinker. Specialist agencies and primary health care workers generally will be perceived as giving advice about drinking, with special reference to how to stop or cut down, so new methods of establishing and maintaining contact need to be explored.

As long as potential clients are motivated to continue drinking, they are unlikely to make contact unless coercion is applied and unlikely to maintain contact unless the agency has something to offer that they, the clients, perceive as being useful. Take for example the distinction between 'advice about drinking' and 'information about alcohol'. Advice about drinking will be well received by individuals who have decided they want to change. It will be avoided by people who want to continue in their drinking. Information about alcohol and its relationship to thiamin deficiency will be useful to individuals who want to continue in the same drinking pattern, but to avoid damaging their central nervous system.

Counsellor style has been shown to affect the drinking pattern of clients: counsellors using non-confrontational approaches, who concur with their clients' accounts, who have an empathic attitude, who use humour and optimism are more successful with problem-drinking clients than are those counsellors who use confrontational approaches, who are incredulous or sarcastic and who argue with clients (Hester and Miller 1989). Additionally counsellors who are experienced, authoritative (about alcohol and its effects), competent (in the delivery of interventions) and flexible (in their ideology) are more likely to maintain contact with clients (Sanchez-Craig 1987).

Showing concern for the client's problems and expressing an interest in maintaining contact by sending friendly and encouraging follow-up letters ('Thank you for coming in, I look forward to seeing you again on Thursday, when we can look at . . .') have been shown to improve the rate at which clients maintain contact with specialist agencies (Hester and Miller 1989).

In addition to counsellor style, a number of *organizational factors* play an important role in encouraging contact with those clients who are yet to be persuaded that contact with a specialist agency may be a good thing.

The physical surroundings communicate to the client what the agency thinks of them and their problem. Shabbiness and carelessly decorated accommodation (notices hanging up with Sellotape, out-of-date announcements of meetings) communicate a very low opinion of themselves to clients. Attention to detail (which is not so much based on absolute resources as the organization and use of resources) communicates a caring attitude and the message that the client is a *valued* person.

Another factor that has been shown to vary the rate at which people attend agencies is waiting time, both from referral to initial contact and actual time spent in the waiting-room. It is now well established that the shorter the time lag between referral and first appointment, the better the chance of attending. A long wait in the waiting-room communicates to clients that their time is not highly valued. To some extent this may be reversed by the offer of an apology when someone is kept waiting. Adequate organization and time management should obviate the need for any waiting time.

Clearly all the above points are applicable to clients in any stage of change and are general examples of good practice. However, where people in pre-contemplation are concerned, there is an above average reluctance to attend, a suspicion of alcohol agencies and what they will do (people often attend *expecting* to be told off) and fear that the valued behaviour, their best available coping strategy, is about to be taken away. With this group, these counsellor and organizational factors take on a higher degree of importance in ensuring contact.

An obvious way to get around some of these problems is to see pre-contemplators in their own homes. Here contact may be just as difficult to establish, but the same counsellor variables apply. Often a neutral contact point in the community, like the GP's surgery or the pub car park, will prove a more acceptable venue.

Initiating a motivational change

Moving out of pre-contemplation and into the first stage of change occurs when conflict about the problem-drinking behaviour is introduced. This happens when thoughts and behaviour are not consistent, for example when heavy drinking conflicts with thoughts of health, responsibility or control. There are a number of 'naturally occurring' ways in which this conflict may be brought into the open. Some of these may be precipitated by the counsellor.

Life events

Sudden changes brought about by unexpected illness, death of a significant other, divorce, or any sudden shock or event which changes the previous balance between the advantages of drinking and the costs of drinking, may precipitate a move into the first stage of change. There is no objectively identifiable list of life events that may bring about this change, since it is the individual's *perception* of what has happened rather than the event itself which may or may not precipitate a change. The counsellor may assist the client in making certain connections between the life event and the problem drinking.

Case study   Moving on from pre-contemplation

Vincent had been drinking on a daily basis for a number of years. When going to football matches at weekends, he would meet his friends and commence drinking as soon as the pubs opened, to 'get a good start'. One Saturday he had been drinking for three hours before the football match commenced. A fire broke out in the stadium and fifty people were burned to death. Vincent stood and watched. Then he went home and locked himself in his room for six days. It was not the horror of watching people burn to death that upset him, it was the fact that he did so without having any feelings at all. He attributed this loss of feeling to the effects of the alcohol, and decided to stop drinking.

In this case study, Vincent could have been relieved that the alcohol had masked any feeling about the scene he was witnessing. Instead, he found his reaction quite unacceptable (watching people die in agony and feeling nothing about it). He made an instant connection between his disturbing reaction to the event and the effects of his drinking and found the 'cost' of his alcohol consumption unacceptably high. The influence of life events are dealt with more fully in Chapter 8.

Maturation

The process of 'growing up' or 'maturing out' of a particular life-style often introduces conflict about the drinking behaviour. A job change or change of partner, two events commonly cited as precipitating change in drinking behaviour, would fall into this category. In the normal course of events, for example, people's drinking patterns often change: when they leave school and get a job (with more money drinking often accelerates); when they leave university and get a job (with more responsibilities drinking often decelerates); when they get married and have children (more demands on time often result in decreasing drinking).

Conflict may be introduced when the old pattern of drinking no longer fits in with the new life-style; the drinking is no longer encouraged and supported in the way it previously was.

Coercion

In the case of life events or maturational processes triggering a change in the drinking behaviour, it is the change in thoughts which precedes a change in behaviour. Coercive measures are an attempt at forcing a behaviour change first, and anticipating a subsequent change in thoughts which will in turn maintain the behaviour change. Court-mandated treatment or education programmes, or attendance under threat of dismissal from a job or divorce, are common examples.

Motivational counselling

Motivational counselling may exploit any or all of the above processes in order to increase the individual's experience of conflict about the drinking.

Where life events or maturational processes occur, the counsellor will assist in the process of changing the client's thoughts about drinking. The aim will be to increase the conflict between thoughts about 'what I do' 'what I want to do' until the behaviour becomes untenable. Where coercive measures have been applied, for example the threat of divorce, dismissal or imprisonment, the behaviour will be changed 'by force'. It is then the role of the therapist to emphasize the positive results of the behaviour change (thoughts like 'I can do it', 'I feel better for doing it') and the negative results of the old behaviour. It will also be an opportunity to explore new ways of dealing with old problems, and an opportunity to experience the benefits of these. Motivational counselling strategies are discussed in full in Chapter 3.

Limiting the damage caused by alcohol

The aim of damage-limitation strategies is to reduce the damage resulting from the drinking in a way that is not conditional upon changing the drinking pattern itself. Damage limitation interventions will now be described more fully.

Damage-limitation interventions

It has been suggested that damage-limitation strategies inhibit or even prevent the possibility of motivational or behaviour change. By 'taking away' the negative consequences of the drinking you take away the need to change. These arguments are based upon two false assumptions:

1 that greater suffering (or the accumulation of negative consequences) will *always* lead to behaviour change
2 that behaviour change will result *only* from increased suffering (or the accumulation of negative consequences).

Theology has its place in the explanation of behaviour changes, but not in the planning of interventions; partial psychological explanations are the inevitable consequence of the long-held idea that you can 'give psychology away' in glossy monthly magazines.

Greater suffering sometimes does lead to behaviour change.

Equally it often leads to accelerated drinking in an attempt to alleviate the suffering. Furthermore, the literature is replete with descriptions of people who gave up problem drinking for positive reasons: love and marriage; a job; a change of peer group; a preferable dependence (Vaillant and Milofsky 1982). When these changes do occur, the less damage the former problem drinker has incurred, the better.

Damage-limitation interventions may be listed under three main headings:

1 those aimed at the individual problem drinker
2 those aimed at third parties who are affected by the individual problem drinker
3 those aimed at the local community, or general population.

Damage-limitation interventions aimed at the individual problem drinker

Periods of enforced abstinence

It is not unusual, during a lengthy and heavy drinking bout, for individuals to reach a stage where they feel too ill to continue or where illness makes continued drinking very difficult. This has little or nothing to do with a decision to change the drinking behaviour except possibly in the very short term. A period of supervised or enforced abstinence in hospital, in a detoxification facility or in a short-stay 'dry' hostel will afford the time to recover physically from the toxic effects of alcohol. A period of total abstinence will enable the body to recover from many of the physical problems caused by the toxic effects of alcohol (see Davies and Raistrick 1981 for a comprehensive list). Long-term disease such as liver cirrhosis, heart disease and damage to the central nervous system may be prevented or delayed by regular periods of enforced abstinence. Detoxification centres, where they have existed, and hospital services with flexible admission criteria have offered just this facility. Agencies for homeless problem drinkers have sometimes organized their services to provide this facility of short-term supervised abstinence, which is not dependent upon a decision to 'give up drinking' or remain abstinent in the long term (St Anne's Alcohol Services in Leeds are an example).

Nutrition

Nutritional deficiencies are not uncommon in problem drinkers; during periods of heavy drinking the diet is likely to be neglected; there is likely to be vomiting; damage to the gastrointestinal system will result in an impaired ability to absorb nutrients; and finally the metabolism of alcohol itself will use up an excess of vital nutrients, such as Vitamin B. Where there is a deficiency of Vitamin B (thiamin), there is a risk of Wernicke's Syndrome which, if untreated, will progress to Korsakoff's Encephalopathy, where the short-term memory becomes irreparably impaired.

Wernicke's Syndrome is treatable by giving immediate (intravenous) thiamin and Korsakoff's Encephalopathy is thus prevented. Since the detection of Wernicke's Syndrome requires a trained medical eye, the administration of thiamin to heavy drinkers routinely by any agency or primary care worker with whom they have contact would be a simple and effective way of preventing the disorder.

More general malnutrition results in an overall weakening of the body's ability to withstand illness and injury; death, as a direct result of malnutrition, is still recorded. It is a risk more generally recognized and catered for in the homeless drinking population. It is equally important to remember to enquire about diet in problem drinkers in more stable domestic situations where it none the less may be neglected.

Change of beverage type

Although it is the alcohol itself that causes problems, some beverages will cause more problems than others. Spirits for example have no nutritional value whatever; their high concentration of absolute alcohol (40–50 per cent by volume) more often causes stomach upsets, and more often results in a higher overall intake of alcohol (it is more difficult to drink spirits slowly). Beer, on the other hand, contains iron and folic acid and does therefore have some nutritional value. Information about the advantages of switching or alternating beverages may well be utilized.

Primary health care

Access to primary health care is often denied to people of no fixed abode, and a number of problem drinkers fall into this category. It may also be avoided by problem drinkers wishing to evade detection or any discussion of their drinking habits. The accessibility of primary health care facilities will depend to some extent upon their preparedness to work with problem drinkers who continue to drink, by exhibiting an accepting attitude towards the person. In other words the environmental and counsellor characteristics noted above are as relevant to the primary health care setting as they are to the specialist agency. Training in the delivery of brief interventions for damage limitation will encourage this accessibility (Tober 1987). Conversely, where primary health care workers have felt it was their responsibility to 'cure' addiction, they have tended to avoid dealing with problem drinkers and maintain a negative attitude to this group.

Accommodation

A great deal of housing provision for problem drinkers was made during the 1970s and 1980s, with an almost universal condition of total abstinence as an admission requirement. A growing recognition that this criterion excluded a large proportion of the target population for whom the provision was designed has resulted in the development of the 'dry house' alternative – the 'wet house'! Although not very attractively named, the provision of this sort of accommodation is based upon the assumption that a large number of problem drinkers will continue to drink, but that it is possible to avert the risks of homelessness none the less. Special provisions are made for the payment of rent, and rules apply to behaviour more generally, rather than the fact or not of drinking. With the provision of such supervised accommodation, other damage-limitation strategies such as the provision of vitamin supplements, a supervised diet, access to primary health care and information about types of beverages and the effects of alcohol may be offered.

Damage-limitation strategies aimed at third parties

Damage to the families of problem drinkers ranges from the immediate effects of intoxication with the attendant risks of violence, accidents and neglect, to the long-term effects of excessive drinking with the attendant risks of loss of income, social rejection and isolation and marital breakdown (Wilson 1982a). Family members develop a whole range of coping strategies to deal with problems of alcohol misuse, and it is the aim of this section to examine the 'successful' coping strategies and to suggest ways of building upon these.

Interventions will be divided into two main headings

1 coping strategies with spouses
2 coping strategies with children.

Coping strategies with spouses

The first step is to establish whether there is a commitment to continue with the marriage. Where the non-problem-drinking spouse – at whom these interventions are aimed – has decided to terminate the marriage, then emotional, practical and guidance to legal support can be offered.

Where the spouse is committed to a continuation of the marriage, the aim of intervention will be

1 the physical protection of the spouse and the children
2 protection of home and income
3 prevention of feelings of helplessness and susceptibility to the behaviour of the drinking spouse
4 improvement in the drinking behaviour.

The next step will be to gain a picture of the effects of drinking on the family:

1 The frequency and duration of drinking: how often does it happen and how long does it go on?
2 Is there intoxication, verbal or physical abuse?
3 Is the family income threatened?
4 Is the home threatened by accident or by lack of finance?
5 What coping strategies does the spouse use for each of the above areas of potential difficulty?

Once a picture of the problems and the spouse's coping strategies has been attained, there are a number of principles which can be applied. Where the spouse's coping strategies are rejecting the *person* who is drinking, the outcome (on all measures of drinking and family hardship) is likely to be poor. Where the coping strategies are accepting the person but rejecting the drinking *behaviour*, the outcome (on measures of drinking and family hardship) is likely to be improved (Orford and Guthrie 1976).

Examples of behaviours which reject the person are refusing to share a bed with him or her; not allowing contact with the children; and excluding the drinker from family activities and decision-making.

Examples of behaviours which reject the drinking but not the person are pouring away the drink; not bringing alcohol into the house; and expressing anger and disapproval when the partner is drinking or is intoxicated.

The spouse is encouraged to continue to use those coping strategies which are consistent with rejecting the drinking and not the drinker, and to abandon the others. Arguments about drinking that occur when the spouse is sober will punish the non-drinking behaviour. Instead positive planning of family activities and domestic management should take place. Consistent disapproval of the drinking when it occurs and approval of non-drinking behaviours should be expressed. A realistic allocation of family roles, such as preparing meals and taking the children to school, rather than paying the rent which gives ready access to funds for drinking, may be devised. The spouse is counselled to persist and to be consistent.

Coping strategy counselling has been carried out in groups for the spouses of problem drinkers where the vicarious advantage of creating a support network for non-drinking partners was achieved (Farid *et al.* 1986). Telephone numbers were exchanged and informal contacts were made outside of the group sessions. Spouses are likely to gain the advantage of feeling less helpless in the face of the problem drinking and more in control of their own and the family life.

Coping strategies with children

There is much scope for developing services for the offspring of problem drinkers in this country as little has been provided to date. The planning of interventions will be based upon the actual and potential risks to offspring, and upon an observation of the environmental and behavioural factors associated with 'survival' in the offspring of problem drinkers.

The risks to the offspring of problem drinkers most commonly identified are:

- alcohol and drug misuse
- records of repeated delinquencies
- learning disabilities
- behaviour disorders (e.g. bed-wetting and problems at school, 'hyperactivity')
- low self-esteem
- external locus of control
- suicidal tendencies.

Physical violence, verbal aggression and observed intoxication increase the risks, as does damaged communication with the mother whether or not she is the problem drinker. As many offspring of problem drinkers do *not* develop problems as those who do. What then are the protective factors?

Environmental factors that have been shown to be associated with offspring who do not develop problems are lack of separation from the primary caretaker in the first two years of life; no additional births in the family in the first two years of life; plenty of attention from the primary caretaker during infancy; and an absence of conflict between the parents during the first two years.

These environmental factors are similar to those identified in children who survive other high-risk family situations. Where they cannot be addressed through contact with the family as a whole and the parents in particular, it will be expedient to arrange nursery places or childminding facilities in order to provide a substitute primary caretaker.

The behavioural characteristics of children who survive have been documented by Werner (1986): the ability to elicit positive attention from the primary caretaker; at least average intelligence; adequate communication skills; an achievement orientation; a positive self-concept; an internal locus of control; and a responsible and caring attitude.

In her research on the impact on children of problem-drinking parents, Wilson (1982b) has found that the children she interviewed were not keen to attend groups for the offspring of problem drinkers. Instead she recommends the development of individual work and points to the scope of alcohol-counselling agencies for developing this work. However, a number of existing community facilities may also be utilized. Youth clubs, after-school clubs, church groups and teachers sensitive to the particular needs of these children may be recruited in the planning of a remedial strategy. Involvement in 'outward bound' activities, sports teams and the variety of youth organizations is a source of enhancing a positive self-concept, an achievement orientation, a responsible and caring attitude and a more internal locus of control. By offering children the opportunity of a focus of activity outside the home, they may come to feel less vulnerable and susceptible to the consequences of heavy drinking.

At an individual level, coping-strategy counselling will be preceded by an assessment of the situation. All information sources should be utilized to gather this information, as a sense of loyalty to the parent may inhibit the child's readiness to discuss the home situation.

Practical considerations include

1 Is the child able to escape in the event of an accident such as fire?
2 Does the child know how to use a telephone and have telephone numbers and coins in order to do so?
3 Does the child have money for bus fares?
4 Does the child know how to prepare a sandwich and where to find food?

5 Does the child have a quiet place to do homework?

Clearly where there is a real threat of violence or neglect, the law (Children and Young Persons Act 1969) provides the machinery for ensuring their protection and safety. But where there is simply an increased risk of emergencies arising, children will feel less vulnerable and helpless where they have some simple problem-solving skills.

Children of problem drinkers are often subject to feelings of excessive responsibility toward the parent with the problem. What can they do to stop them drinking, or to look after them generally? Though their responsibilities might be appropriately extended as they grow into their late teens, for younger children direct and simple advice on what to do in an emergency, which is designed to protect themselves, may help in clarifying what is expected of them.

Emotional and social considerations include

1 Does the child have special friends at school or elsewhere?
2 Is there an extended family or other significant person to whom the child can turn?
3 Does the child have adequate opportunities to play?
4 Does the child attend school regularly?
5 How does the child feel about the problem-drinking parent?

Again, where problems reach extreme proportions, the law may be invoked to take protective action. Persistent non-school attendance would be an example. The children of problem drinkers may have difficulties with school attendance due to lack of appropriate clothes to wear, lack of bus fares, or requests to stay home and take care of ill parents or younger siblings. These problems may arise only on an occasional basis, and not frequently enough to invoke the law. (Arguably the act of invoking the law in itself introduces a new range of risks to the child.) They may none the less be an appropriate focus of remedial intervention.

Embarrassment about the home situation may result in social isolation. Children may be encouraged to see friends at clubs and meetings outside the home; these will provide the additional advantages of a place to play and opportunities to make supportive contacts with potential significant others like youth leaders and play-group leaders.

Children may feel angry or let down with the problem-drinking parent – boys being more likely to indulge in delinquent behaviour as a result, and girls being more likely to develop emotional disorders and to harm themselves. An opportunity to express this anger in a forum where there are no repercussions for the child or parent may be provided by a counsellor in a specialist agency.

Cast study   Stephanie's four children

Samantha is 12; she does well at school, she is in the hockey team and she has friends with whom she goes out at the weekends. She gets very angry with her mother when Stephanie is obviously drinking and reacts to this by going round to see a friend where she will often stay for tea and overnight.

Nicholas is 10; he is a quiet boy who gets by without comment at school. He always comes straight home and plays with his younger sisters. He also spends time alone in his bedroom playing with cars and reading comics.

Emily is an entirely average and boisterous 6 year old. She gives her father a daily report on whether her mother has been drinking or not, saying additionally whether she is 'ill', 'upset' or simply 'asleep'.

Sarah is 2; she doesn't look like the rest of the family. She has a 'flattened'-looking face, with eyes set far apart and a wide stretch between her nose and mouth. Her joints are not properly formed and she cannot stand up or walk. She is very small for her age and does not speak except for one or two words.

The youngest daughter has already been damaged, probably by the mother's drinking during pregnancy. The abnormalities she shows (characteristic of foetal alcohol effects) in themselves place her at risk for the development of further problems in the future (she will have low intelligence, continue to show delayed development progress, is likely to be a 'difficult' child and therefore not to elicit positive attention from her primary caretakers). Moreover, since the mother continues to drink she is unlikely to provide her with the special attention and stimulation she requires. Daily attendance at a nursery or children's centre would be the optimal course to take.

The son would be another legitimate focus of attention. He feels excessive responsibility for his mother's drinking and returns home from school to look after his sisters; he also feels a degree of shame and embarrassment which results in social isolation. It would be highly appropriate to arrange involvement in an after-school activity with peers and for him to be seen outside the family to offer the opportunity of expressing some of his feelings about the drinking.

Gillian Tober

It would appear that the main risk to Samantha will be of developing a drinking problem herself. She seems at the moment to have good coping skills to deal with the situation, but she lacks the opportunity to develop a 'normal' attitude to alcohol and in the future 'sensible' drinking skills. School education programmes, peer-group influences and the non-problem-drinking father will all have an important role to play.

The problems likely to occur in the offspring of problem drinkers are not dissimilar to those likely to occur in the offspring of other problem groups. Remedial interventions are well advanced in some areas (e.g. headstart nurseries, surrogate primary caretakers, 'outward bound' activities). The task is one of identifying the offspring of problem drinkers as a target group worthy of intervention, and applying these well-established remedial interventions to them.

Damage-limitation interventions aimed at the local community

Recommendations for local community action in the prevention of alcohol problems have been made and acted upon (Tether and Robinson 1986; Robinson *et al.* 1989). It is not the intention of this section to repeat these, but rather to distil out those initiatives which fall specifically into the category of damage limitation strategies (i.e. they are designed to reduce the damage without *necessarily* reducing the drinking itself) and which are amenable to action on the part of the local alcohol agency. Inclusion of members of the alcohol industry, the magistracy and the police on the local alcohol/drug advisory committee creates a forum for debate and planning action in co-operation with the local agency and relevant primary workers.

Some UK examples and suggestions of initiatives designed to reduce the extent of alcohol-related accidents and violence follow.

1 In Leicestershire an alcohol-agency-based prevention officer advises pub landlords on interior design conducive to creating a calm atmosphere and reducing the likelihood of accidents and violence (Robinson *et al.* 1989).

2 In Humberside an early warning system in licensed premises is used to give police notice of developing alcohol-related disturbances (Robinson *et al.* 1989).

3 The variety of non-drinking-driver schemes, which have been devised by brewers to reduce the incidence of driving over the permitted limit, have ensured the availability of a driver to take people home from the pub. Beer mats, information packs, badges

and hats (chauffeurs' caps) were all used to publicize these schemes. A principle well worth remembering is that where behaviour change is desired, education about what needs to be done, backed up by a negative sanction for non-compliance, will be much more effective when the means for making the behaviour change are instantly available.

4 The laws against selling alcohol to and purchasing alcohol for intoxicated people could be more regularly enforced as a result of co-operative endeavours between the relevant agencies.

The planning of such initiatives on a local basis will be facilitated by the existence and utilization of a local policy for the prevention of alcohol problems (Anderson 1989). Such a policy will embrace the whole gamut of harm-reduction strategies – whether these are based in the work-place, in local commerce, law-enforcement agencies or generic and specialist treatment agencies. The policy creates a forum for discussion and planning, and supplies the much-needed legitimation of and support for the resulting initiatives.

Further issues

Recent texts on alcohol interventions have begun to include descriptions of people in pre-contemplation, and methods for working with them (Miller and Heather 1986; Hester and Miller 1989). However, these interventions are aimed specifically at the decision-making process and at changing the motivation of the person in pre-contemplation.

Failure to achieve this motivational change results in the continuing frustrations of counsellers who deal with this group of problem drinkers. These frustrations in turn result in the cultivation of negative attitudes, where pre-contemplators are described as people who 'lie about their drinking', 'deny that they have a problem', or are 'unmotivated to change'. In an attempt to keep the counsellor's own attribution system intact, individuals in pre-contemplation are blamed for their refusal to comply with treatment and ultimately excluded from it or written off as a 'treatment failure'. But there is another way of looking at it. The frustrations experienced by specialist and primary counsellors alike are the product of continually setting inappropriate goals. This chapter is an attempt to show that many of the factors causing a change of mind about drinking are beyond the scope of the counsellor to effect. They can be exploited when they occur, but few opportunities exist to introduce change factors at this stage.

The introduction of damage-limitation interventions for people

Gillian Tober

in pre-contemplation has many advantages. The goals of these interventions are more modest, but more realistic. *Something* can be done. Furthermore, problem drinkers can be engaged in a 'therapeutic' (in the sense of beneficial) relationship, on the basis of being offered a service that is perceived by them as being useful. Finally, treatment outcome figures will be greatly improved by deducting from the relapse rates all of those people who never decided to change!

References

Anderson, P. (1989) 'Health authority policies for the prevention of alcohol problems', *British Journal of Addiction* 84, 2: 203–9.

Davies, I. and Raistrick, D. (1981) *Dealing with Drink*, London: BBC Publications.

Farid, B., Sherini, M.E. and Raistrick, D.S. (1986) 'Cognitive group therapy for wives of alcoholics', *Drug and Alcohol Dependence* 4: 349–58.

Hester, R. and Miller W.R. (eds) (1989) *Handbook of Alcoholism Treatment Approaches: Effective Approaches*, Oxford: Pergamon.

Miller, W.R. and Heather, N. (eds) (1986) Treating Addictive Behaviours: Processes of Change, New York: Plenum Press.

Orford, J. and Guthrie, S. (1976) 'Coping behaviour used by wives of alcoholics: a preliminary investigation', in G. Edwards, M.A.H. Russell, D. Hawks and M. MacCafferty (eds) *Alcohol Dependence and Smoking Behaviour*, London: Saxon House.

Robinson, D., Tether, P. and Teller, J. (1989) *Local Action on Alcohol Problems*, London: Routledge.

Sanchez-Craig, M. (1987) 'Short-term treatment: conceptual and practical issues', paper presented at *Fourth International Conference on the Treatment of Addictive Behaviours*, Norway.

Tether, P. and Robinson, D. (1986) *Preventing Alcohol Problems: A Guide to Local Action*, London: Tavistock.

Tober, G. (1987) 'Training in addiction', paper presented at *Seventh International Conference on Alcohol Problems*, Liverpool.

Vaillant, G.E. and Milofsky, E.S. (1982) 'Natural history of male alcoholism', *Archives of General Psychiatry* 39: 127–33.

Werner, E.E. (1986) 'Resilient offspring of alcoholics: a longitudinal study from birth to age 18', *Journal of Studies on Alcohol* 47, 1: 34–40.

Wilson, C. (1982a) 'The family', in Camberwell Council on Alcoholism (eds) *Women and Alcohol*, London: Camberwell Council on Alcoholism.

—— (1982b) 'The impact on children', in J. Orford and J. Harwin (eds) *Alcohol and the Family*, London: Croom Helm.

Chapter three

Helping the unsure

Steve Baldwin

What is the contemplation stage?

Clients who have recognized the existence of a problem behaviour, but who have not yet taken action, are in a stage of *contemplation*. Specifically they are *thinking* rather than *doing*. As with other addictive behaviours, such as smoking, clients may remain as 'thinkers' for many weeks or months. For some drinking clients, this transition into an 'action' phase may take more than twelve months. Equally some clients may decide not to take action, and choose to continue their existing drinking patterns. This exit from the sequence of pre-contemplation – contemplation – action – maintenance – relapse may require a shift of perceptual set (e.g. 'I am not prepared to change my drinking habits, although my partner has threatened to leave me if I continue to drink'). Other clients continue to contemplate change, waiting for the 'right moment' to occur to try again.

While some drinking clients will enter the stage of contemplation from a period of pre-contemplation, others will re-enter this stage following a relapse from a previously unsuccessful change attempt. Such clients have experienced relapse after unsuccessful main-tenance, and therefore will bring a different kind of challenge for counsellors. In particular, these clients may have been sensitized to a previous form of intervention or assistance, which precludes its subsequent use with that client. (Drinking diaries, for example, may be a weak method of behaviour change for some clients, who will require more potent methods of self-control during subsequent attempts.)

Change processes and change stages

Verbal processes of change (awareness-raising; catharsis; choosing) are used most often during the stages of contemplation (Prochaska and DiClemente 1982). In particular, a cathartic experience (e.g. expression of emotions or feelings) may bridge the gap between contemplation and determination, before taking action. Such an emotional experience (e.g. a fight with a spouse or best friend) may precipitate a change of habit patterns. Thus, while behavioural patterns are more important once clients have committed themselves to change, *verbal processes (talking) are most important in preparing clients for action during the stage of contemplation.*

While specific events (e.g. contact with other persons) may produce the change from contemplation to action, 'developmental processes' also may move people into a new stage in life. For example, much behavioural reform (with shifts from contemplation to action) is observed as adults approach 'middle age' at 40. Other psychologically important markers (e.g. childbirth, marriage) may also precipitate change. A successful transition between stages will require restructuring of beliefs and values, as well as acquisition of new behaviour patterns.

One conclusion from research completed with clients with other addictive behaviour problems is that people should be viewed as potent 'agents of change'; most problem drinkers resolve their drink problems without assistance from counsellors. Many clients are highly selective about their responses to counsellors who 'motivate' them into the next stage of change. Indeed, some clients with drink problems may resist change attempts due to differences of understanding with the counsellor about which stage of change has been reached. Directive, action-oriented alcohol counsellors may find clients who are still in contemplation (and therefore not yet ready for action) highly resistant to change attempts. Equally counsellors who specialize in 'raising awareness' may find 'action-oriented' clients resistant to their interventions.

To avoid attrition (drop-out from counselling), counsellors should check that clients whom they perceive to be 'thinkers' and not 'doers' are truly in the stage of contemplation. Alcohol counsellors who misclassify 'doers' as 'thinkers' may risk delays in the change process.

Features of the contemplation stage

Contemplation is characterized by an **awareness** by clients that they have a drink problem. This will require an admission by the individual that a behaviour (or set of behaviours) which previously has been considered normal and usual is now viewed as 'the problem'. As might be expected, this admission may induce distress, due to some fundamental challenges to personal attitudes, beliefs or values.

Clients who are contemplators have not yet made personal decisions to take action, but may seek new information to help solve their problems. As yet, no actual commitment to change has occurred via new or alternative behaviours. With some drinkers, the stage of contemplation can become prolonged, due to idiosyncratic features of the individual. Some clients, for example, will have become 'trapped' in obsessional thinking styles (e.g. rumination or compulsive thoughts) and may find it difficult to break out of these restrictive belief systems. In particular, such clients may believe that if they spend enough time dwelling on the problem, it will go away, or that enough information will be collected to provide a 'perfect solution'. This irrational belief system may perpetuate information-seeking in clients (or alcohol counsellors) beyond reasonable time limits, and delay progression towards the 'action' stage.

The duration of the stage of contemplation will co-vary both with the nature, intensity, duration and severity of the client's drinking problems, and with the skills of the alcohol counsellor. The skilled counsellor will make an accurate appraisal of the individual needs of each client, and will be able to resist the stereotyped application of 'standard packages'. Not all clients, for example, will respond positively to the attempts of counsellors to provide written information via leaflets; some clients will resist such attempts at 'teaching' using educational materials.

Most clients in the stage of contemplation who attend for counselling are ready to talk about their problems, and will be seeking reassurance and confirmation from the counsellor that their problems can be resolved. In general, they will be receptive to the provision of articles, books, leaflets and other educational materials about alcohol or drinking. Despite a readiness to talk, however, there is **inaction** until more insight has occurred. Personal distress may be an obstacle to a further shift into an action stage, due to a realization about the likely loss of rewards previously associated with drinking. Also, there may be particular concerns about whether or not reform attempts will be successful. The challenge for counsellors is to gauge the 'readiness' of problem drinkers to move from contemplation into action. Clients may become stuck at any stage of change; should this occur, the counsellor should aim to discover what is required to unfreeze the client from 'chronic contemplation'.

Objectives

What to do/what not to do

Skilled counselling with problem drinkers will require a full appreciation of the **nature** of the contemplation stage. In particular, counsellors should realize that contemplators may need assistance with attitude change, rather than direct work with their drinking behaviours. Social and environmental action (e.g. helping relationships; social liberation) or educational (e.g. awareness-raising; dramatic relief) are likely to help shift the client to the action stage.

The stage of contemplation will involve consideration by drinkers of the scope and impact of their problems. New information may be used to consider the relative advantages and disadvantages of unmodified drinking patterns; this information will be essential to the self-re-evaluation, which occurs during contemplation. This re-evaluation involves consideration of the **meaning** (and role) of alcohol in the life of the drinker, as well as a probable shift in the balance of positive and negative values attached to specific behaviours. In particular, an increase in negative valuation of the problem behaviour, as well as a positive valuation about self-control and coping skills, will enhance this shift. This can be achieved by directing clients to consider specific aspects of their drinking (e.g. 'Tell me some of the things that bother you about your drinking' or 'In what ways do you now begin to feel more able to take control of your drinking?').

These processes of awareness-raising and re-evaluation will produce either a decision to take action towards personal change, or a decision that change is too difficult, ill-timed or inappropriate. A 'decision not to change' may seem irrational or illogical to the counsellor, who is well-placed to see the apparent need for personal change and reform. Both decisions should be respected, however. The decision not to change is valid for the individual drinker, especially given the need to respect responsibility and self-determination. Counsellors should recognize that, despite knowledge of likely consequences of continued problem drinking, some clients will not adopt rational or logical views. Individual clients often arrive for counselling or therapy *to contemplate change*, and *not to take action*. Counsellors should beware of attempts to shift drinking clients from a 'decision not to change'.

How to do it

Clients with drinking problems may have other problems in other areas of their life, including interpersonal (between several people), family, and intrapersonal (within the person) difficulties. Often the drinking problem is a **multi-level** problem, which will require interventions at each level to resolve the difficulty successfully. The skilled counsellor will aim to assess the client's problems at a range of levels and evaluate the stage of change at each level. Usually the drinking behaviour will be the central focus of the counsellor. None the less, consideration is required of other related aspects of the client's life (e.g. health; housing; employment; relationships; recreation). Skilled counselling may also require a focus on these or other themes during the stage of contemplation.

An appreciation of interventions which are potent during contemplation will assist the counsellor to avoid use of non-explanatory terms such as 'motivation' and 'recidivism'.

Counsellors may risk non-efficient use of their energies, due to (mis)application of potentially useful techniques at the incorrect stage. Behaviour change strategies (such as drink diaries) risk **misapplication**, if offered to clients at the stage of contemplation, when verbal techniques which focus on attitude change are more appropriate. Skilled counsellors should be able to think and intervene using a comprehensive set of techniques.

Clients who are in the contemplation stage are most open to awareness-raising interventions, such as observations, confrontations and interpretations (Prochaska and DiClemente 1983). Drinking clients in contemplation are more likely to make use of 'bibliotherapy' (e.g. self-help books) and other educational materials. Information generally will help these clients to re-evaluate themselves. For clients whose drinking has been central to their self-image, such re-evaluation will require a fundamental personal reappraisal. These clients may ask themselves (and/or their counsellor): 'Will I prefer myself more if I cut down my drinking?' or more frequently, 'Won't I lose all my friends if I stop drinking?' Counsellors should be prepared to enable their clients to resolve these fundamental questions for themselves, and not provide stereotyped reassurances. The skilled counsellor will assist clients to make their own informed decisions, using adequate information.

Progression from contemplation into action

Once clients have become 'contemplators', further insight and self-understanding may be required for progress into an **action** stage. The type of insight will depend on the nature of their problem, and the level of change required. For some clients, a **behavioural analysis** (determination of the functional relationships between drinking, and its cues and consequences) may be sufficient to

Steve Baldwin

promote self-awareness and self-understanding. For other clients, whose drinking problems are interwoven into relationship discord (e.g. drinking to 'resolve' marital difficulties), different insights about interpersonal factors will be required.

Case Study Being a contemplator

Ken is a 22-year-old man who was referred by the district (magistrates') court for assessment for an Alcohol Education Course. At the time of referral, he was drinking three or four days each week, with an average intake of between 100 and 120 units during these sessions. Ken started the assessment interview by saying: 'I don't mind answering your questions, but I won't be going on the course, because I don't have a problem'. This was countered with: 'It's not for me to tell you if you have a problem or not; it's up to you to decide that for yourself. Let's take a look at your drinking and see how you're doing just now'.

During the interview, it became clear that Ken had been thinking about his drinking. An examination of his drinking history indicated a steady increase during the previous four years; his drinking had increased again recently due to overtime payments for labouring work. His offending history indicated five convictions in the previous two years for public order and property offences. The most recent police arrest followed an incident when he had fallen through a fish and chip shop window during a street fight.

A detailed behavioural analysis was used to examine the functional relationship between Ken's drinking and offending. For each offence, Ken was asked about the preceding events. In particular, he was asked to focus on whether or not drinking had occurred prior to the offence. Further questions about *whom* he was with, *doing what*, *where*, and *in what way* produced this summary statement from the interview:

'Ken, what you seem to be saying is that you've been lifted five times before, and again last month. Each time you've been caught by the police, it's been after a long drinking session. Every time, you've been drinking for at least five hours; you've never been lifted before half-past ten, and always on a Friday or Saturday night. Gary has always been with you, and usually John as well. You've always been caught in the High Street, or in the Royal Terrace. Every time it's been because you've been making noise in the street, or because you've damaged someone's property on the way home. What do *you* think? *Is* there a connection between your drinking habits and getting into trouble with the police?'

This summary was used as a springboard to confront Ken with

his drinking habits. Despite a clear functional relationship between heavy drinking sessions and subsequent offending behaviours, Ken had not been aware of this. When asked, he had attributed his arrests and detention to a bias amongst police officers. This belief was also challenged, and Ken was asked to 'plot' his offences on a city map. His six offences formed a straight line between a city-centre pub and his flat.

Ken's lack of insight and distorted belief system were systematically challenged during the interview. His drink-related physical health and social problems were reattributed to alcohol consumption. Ken was assisted to view his problems as an *understandable pattern* rather than a *random set of unconnected events*. He subsequently decided to attend an Alcohol Education Course to help him with his drinking and offending behaviours.

The effective transition from contemplation into action may require a raising of awareness, as well as self-re-evaluation. In addition to interventions such as observation, confrontation and interpretation, 'values-clarification' techniques may assist clients to prepare for effective personal action. Such techniques are based on a skilled approach to a consideration of the balance between the 'pros and cons' of drinking. The challenge for counsellors is to assist clients to generate accurate, comprehensive lists of the advantages and disadvantages of personal reform. Such change may be enhanced via the use of 'motivational interviewing' techniques.

Therapeutic interventions

Motivational interviewing techniques

Traditional accounts of human motivation have attributed most properties of behaviour change to the characteristics of individuals. Such models have included 'attributional biases', which have apportioned *credit* to successful behaviour change programmes, and *failure* to personal qualities of problem drinkers. In particular, unsuccessful programme implementation has often been blamed on to deficiencies within the client.

One contemporary motivational model has proposed an alternative for this traditional perspective (Miller 1983). The concept of 'denial' has been reframed to include an explicit consideration of counsellor characteristics. Traditional models have located denial within the drinker, to explain resistance to behaviour change

45

attempts. An alternative explanation has relocated the origins of 'denial' by clients as a function of counsellor style. Specifically clients may adopt an opposite position to the counsellor, because of more fundamental aspects of social interaction. The presentation of a strong argument by the counsellor (e.g. for the client to stop drinking) may generate a counter-argument by the client (to continue to drink). This may be less a function of the client's views on drinking, and more a function of the fundamental nature of human beings. Direct argumentation (e.g. 'You should stop drinking') is ineffective in attitude change, and may be the worst way to try to change the opinion of a drinking client. Continued pressure from the counsellor rather may increase the commitment of clients to their initial position.

The contemporary perspective of 'motivational interviewing' (Miller 1983; Miller *et al.* 1987) has proposed four key principles for clients to 'talk themselves' into behaviour change. First, **self-labelling** by the client (e.g. 'I am a problem drinker') is not viewed as a prerequisite for behaviour change. There is no evidence that such self-labelling is associated with improved outcome.

Second, clients are encouraged to take **self-responsibility** for their problems; it is for the client to decide what work is required. It is for the counsellor to promote a 'view of reality' with accuracy and clarity, but the client should decide what is required. A decision that 'change is not required' *is* viable. The drinker should make the final decision about change or no change, and should not merely agree with the counsellor's viewpoint.

Third, clients are encouraged to attribute to themselves the potential (and credit) for change; this is consonant with the view that drinkers are **active agents**, responsible for their own behaviour. Drinking is viewed as a personal choice; responsibility for this cannot (and should not) be taken by the counsellor.

Fourth, the challenge for the counsellor is to encourage clients to recognize inconsistency, or **dissonance**, within themselves. This requires clients to become aware of discrepancies between their personal beliefs, attitudes or values, and their actual behaviour. Counselling may require clients to make such realizations explicit, via insights about themselves (e.g. 'Drinking and driving is not just illegal, it's wrong for *me*' or 'I'd like to think I can hold my tongue, as well as my drink, but I *know* I embarrassed myself at that party last weekend').

Successful motivational interviewing will require the achievement of specific goals, including increased self-esteem; increased feelings of personal coping; increased dissonance (via an awareness of the discrepancy between attitudes, beliefs, values and/or behaviour); and reduced dissonance toward positive behaviour change (so that the client will be more likely to change negative drinking behaviours).

Such a goal may be achieved via **affirmation** of the client by the counsellor, from accurate empathic statements (e.g. 'I know it is difficult for you to reduce your drinking, and you've been working hard at that'). **Reflection** may be used to highlight positive coping statements by clients. It can also be used to restructure or reframe the content from a client, to offer a different interpretation of the situation (e.g. 'You've mentioned your spouse several times now; perhaps you feel he/she is related to your drinking in some way?').

Increased self-awareness will require the active involvement of the client. This is based on the belief that clients should talk themselves into change, via **self-motivational** statements. Skilled counsellors can assist this change with specific questions (e.g. 'I know what you *like* about your drinking. Which things about it cause you *problems*?'). Similarly the advanced counsellor may use **paradoxical** techniques to assist drinkers to talk themselves into change; this requires the counsellor to adopt a 'devil's advocate' position (e.g. 'I'm not at all sure you really do have a drink problem. Perhaps you feel as if everything is OK after all?'; or even 'Have you considered drinking *more* alcohol?').

Another aspect of motivational interviewing is based on the provision of **objective feedback**, based on norms (i.e. what is usual for most people). This may involve the administration of simple assessment techniques to determine the different components of the individual's drinking. This may include provision of consumption data measured in standard units of drinking; blood alcohol levels; liver function test (LFT) results and neuropsychological measures. The skill in motivational interviewing is to give objective feedback about drinking (e.g. 'Your weekly level of consumption of forty-five units is more than twice the maximum level considered to be safer limits by many experts') rather than to overwhelm the client with a confrontational style. The skilled counsellor will invite clients to 'talk themselves' into change (e.g. 'What do you suppose all this means?') rather than to state a conclusion as a *fait accompli*.

The counsellor will aim to summarize the present state of the client, via accurate reflections and feedback. This will include any ambivalent statements the client has made about change (e.g. 'Let me see if I have understood you. You have given plenty of reasons to cut down your drinking, but you still have some reservations. You seem to be on the brink of a decision. Is that how it feels for you?').

Discussion of alternatives

Many drinking clients will view their alternatives as narrow, dual-option choices between equally unattractive outcomes (e.g. 'Either I carry on with this crazy drinking pattern, or I have to stop completely – now!'). The counsellor can assist clients to increase their openness to re-evaluation, and to ensure that conflict about change is enhanced, via consideration of the positive outcomes of reform. Counsellors often have extensive experience of their own attempts to resolve their drinking problems, and these experiences should be incorporated in decisions about what to include (or exclude) in subsequent change attempts. In the stage of contemplation, the counsellor should assist clients to review a broad range of alternatives, to make an informed choice about subsequent action. Some clients will have adopted dualistic, opposite or extreme views which will require appropriate confrontation (e.g. 'You seem to think you have to maintain your extremely high levels of drinking at sixty units per week, or stop at once. Aren't there any other options for you?').

In summary, the counsellor does not moralize, or threaten the client, but rather leaves individuals to make their own decisions about change. Responsibility for choice remains with the client. The counsellor does not provide 'cookbook' solutions to the complex problems of the client, and does not reject clients if they reject the counsellor's suggestions. Strategies to increase awareness and affirmation by the counsellor, together with a consideration of possible alternatives, will assist the client's progress from contemplation to action.

Drinkers' Check-Up (DCU)

One recent extension of this work on motivational interviewing has been the development of the *Drinkers' Check-up* (Miller *et al.* 1987). The DCU has been derived from a health-promotion model, using a battery of measures sensitive to the early effects of alcohol on physical health and psychological functioning. The DCU includes a structured interview about drinking patterns; blood tests; neuropsychological tests (to detect possible early brain damage); 'collateral' interviews (with other persons who are close to the drinker); alcohol use inventory. These measures have been selected to provide a comprehensive overview of the individual's current functioning.

Possible applications of the DCU include health screening (for routine preventive work); selection and matching (to filter drinking clients into appropriate programmes); self-assessment (to promote self-referrals amongst the population of at-risk drinkers); research/ evaluation (to provide routine information about outcomes of interventions). In particular, the DCU may help to provide a standardized assessment tool to assist clients in contemplating action; the provision of feedback about the effects of their drinking may be sufficient to help clients to make a transition between stages.

While it is a recent (mostly unevaluated) development, the DCU remains a very promising example of a so-called 'minimal intervention' for use by alcohol counsellors with drinking clients. Brief screening interviews, such as DCU, can be offered routinely in settings where clients usually have limited contact with 'the system' (e.g. GP surgeries; employee alcohol services; social work departments; non-medical or medical health services). Such 'minimal motivational interventions' could be offered to people seeking help, to enable transition from contemplation into action.

Barriers to change

The contemporary model of change has predicted that, following a period of contemplation, clients with addictive behaviour problems either will exit from the model (having decided that 'no change' is best), or will progress into an 'action' stage, via determination of a commitment to behaviour change. While many clients with addictive behaviour problems will successfully make this transition into 'action', some will not overcome potential barriers to change.

These barriers may be based on a fear of the unknown, and unresolved doubts about not being in control. Thus, while drinking may be 'out of control', it may nevertheless enable the drinker to exert much control over the behaviour of others (e.g. family, spouse, partner). It may also provide the source of much avoidance behaviour by the drinker (e.g. intoxication providing a means to avoid resolution of financial problems). The potential for the shift into action, to resolve problem drinking, therefore may produce major threats to the 'psychological safety' of clients. These threats (perceived or actual) will be maximal when the client feels subjectively that change has been *imposed* from an external source (e.g. a family member; an alcohol counsellor).

Another barrier for a transition to the action stage may be the time duration in contemplation; clients may ruminate and dwell on the negative aspects of change, which will increase their apprehension. Counsellors therefore should aim to determine the time duration that referred drinkers have already spent in contemplation. People with addictive behaviour problems may spend up to two years in contemplation (Prochaska and DiClemente 1982, 1986); counsellors should check with clients their previous time spent in contemplation. Lengthy prior time spent in this stage may indicate specific interventions to promote client advancement towards action. Specifically clients with a long history in contemplation may require more direct, powerful interventions (e.g. multiple techniques of confrontation) to facilitate change. *A lengthy duration in contemplation should alert counsellors to consider advanced techniques of behaviour change.*

Reasons for 'no change'

A decision of 'no change' may be a valid (although not necessarily desirable) response to the stage of contemplation by some clients (Miller 1983). While clients in contemplation have the right to determine their own future, and should be encouraged to take full responsibility for this decision, other factors may produce a negative response to change attempts. For this reason, counsellors should be aware of several variables (not specific to clients, but rather a function of counsellor–client interactions) which may contribute to the failure of behaviour change attempts.

Behaviour change may not succeed for various reasons:

1 the purpose and reasons for change have not been made clear, resulting in a lack of focus and direction (i.e. the client will not know when 'success' has been achieved)
2 non-involvement in planning, resulting in lack of commitment, or destructive behaviours
3 no reason to change, producing passive acceptance of counsellor suggestions
4 costs too high/rewards too low, where sacrifices are not outweighed by benefits which may occur
5 high fear of failure (perceived or actual)
6 culture ignored, when the counsellor does not confer sufficient value and respect for the client's existing skills and knowledge
7 lack of respect or trust between the counsellor and the client
8 poor communication, when the counsellor does not convey adequate and accurate feedback about the client's progress during the contemplation stage.

Successful change

A successful transition from contemplation into action will require an accurate identification and definition of problem behaviours.

Typically this is based on the cessation of negative behaviours and the introduction of more positive strategies; both situations may involve the acquisition of new skills and repertoires. The successful transition towards an 'action' stage will require the counsellor to consider features of the client such as readiness; commitment; the use of small, manageable steps; familiarity with the techniques or procedures; use of energy to achieve manageable goals. When working with a client who is in contemplation, the counsellor should consider the novelty of techniques used; the complexity of changes required by the client; the degree to which success depends on others (e.g. spouse, best friend); previous history of success or failure; and client vulnerability to external influences. Skilled alcohol counselling should incorporate consideration of these factors, which may influence success outcomes.

Competence curves

People in change situations (e.g. between the stages of contemplation to action) experience 'competence curves'. Specifically there is some evidence that people respond to change in a similar fashion, irrespective of the nature of the change, and the individual people involved (see Figure 3.1).

Although individuals progress through the curve at different rates, some people may become 'stuck' at a particular stage. Specific interventions (e.g. education, acquisition of a new skill) may be required to move the person along the curve. Thus for some people, knowledge about the curve will be sufficient for progress; others will require specific assistance from counsellors. Drinking clients who experience simultaneous change in several areas of their 'life events' (e.g. marital breakdown; death of a close relative; birth; employment difficulties; financial problems) may require additional assistance to make progress (see Chapter 8).

Self-help methods

Many problem drinkers do not use formal counselling or therapeutic services, but initiate and manage their self-change without assistance (Miller 1983; Miller *et al.* 1987). While the true percentage may be unknown, survey reports suggest that many problem drinkers can resolve their difficulties with no outside help, or via 'minimal interventions' (i.e. brief contact with therapist or therapeutic materials).

The development of self-help manuals has produced interest amongst both evaluators and fieldwork practitioners. Alcohol

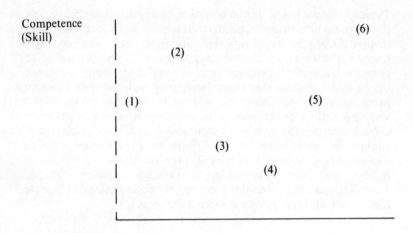

Competence
(Skill)

(1) = immobilization shock
(2) = denial ('this is not really happening')
(3) = incompetence awareness ('I can't cope')
(4) = reality acceptance ('yes it's different')
(5) = testing new approaches
(6) = integration of old and new skills

Figure 3.1 Competence curve of individuals expressing change

counsellors have used these manuals to complement (or replace) more intensive, lengthy contact with their clients. In particular, counsellors have used these materials with clients in contemplation, to provide a combination of information, education, self-assessment and feedback.

Case study   Moving on from contemplation

Sam is a 25-year-old postgraduate student. His course required both daytime work and evening studies. During the week, he would not drink alcohol at all, partly due to driving up to 120 miles every day. At the weekend, however, he would drink on Friday nights and on Saturdays, although not on Sundays.

Sam's consumption on Friday nights included four or five pints of beer, with occasional single or double measures of spirits. During Saturday lunchtime he would drink another four or five pints, and then another six or seven pints during the evening. Sometimes ordinary-strength lager was substituted by strong lager. Sam did not think he had a drink problem, although some of his friends had commented on his weekend drinking pattern. Due to some recent drink-related physical health problems (e.g. stomach upsets, diarrhoea and headaches) however, Sam had begun to think about cutting back his drinking.

Some weekends, Sam would drive, having previously been drinking, during late Saturday night and early Sunday morning. While he might wait several hours between stopping drinking and starting to drive, he would still sometimes drive when intoxicated. While Sam had contemplated the consequences of police apprehension for drinking and driving, this had not impacted on his behaviour. This pattern had been established during a period of twelve months.

One Saturday night, Sam had been drinking with two friends until closing time. They decided to visit the next town ten miles away. Sam offered to drive, although he had been drinking for the previous four hours, and also at lunchtime the same day. Sam drove ten miles without incident, although at excessive speed along a fast straight road. At a roundabout at the end of this road, however, he clipped a kerb on making his exit, causing a loud noise underneath the car. While Sam retained control and continued the journey, his friends were silent. Sam cut short the trip, and they returned home.

The next day, on reflection of the incident, Sam imagined the consequences of having lost control of the car the previous night, or having hit a pedestrian. As a result, he decided not to drive at all if he had been drinking, and immediately took further action to reduce his drinking.

Most self-help manuals share fundamental principles of design, and include sections with education (e.g. information about units of alcohol); self-assessment (e.g. recording of daily drinking); goal-setting (e.g. identification of more appropriate drinking levels by volume); self-monitoring (e.g. feedback to self about progress); self-management (e.g. skills to cope with difficult situations involving alcohol). While most self-help manuals have been designed for the 'general population' of drinkers (e.g. Robertson and Heather 1985), some have been developed for more specific populations, such as offenders (e.g. Baldwin *et al.* 1988; McMurran 1987).

Review

Clients in contemplation are engaged in a set of comparisons between their present stage and a more ideal condition. This

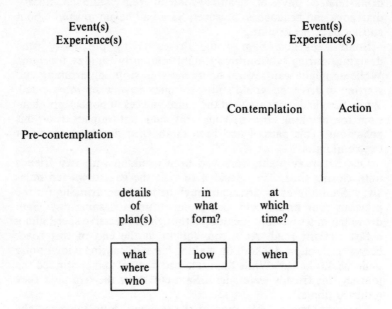

Figure 3.2 Transition from pre-contemplation to contemplation to action

process will usually have been prompted by some event or experience during a previous stage of pre-contemplation, where drinking was not viewed as problematic. As a result of newly acquired information, the client will have shifted into a stage of contemplation; the challenge for the counsellor is to propel the client toward *action*.

Counsellors will need to work with clients through the transition stage of contemplation, via commitment to a plan for action (see Figure 3.2). This will require specific information about in what way(s) the change will be achieved; who will be involved in the plan; and where the plan will be executed. Skilled counsellors will work with clients to formulate a plan for change; the probabilities of successful intervention will be increased by the inclusion of detailed information about the 'what, where and who' of plans for change.

In addition, counsellors should work with clients to include details of how (i.e. in what form) the plan will be achieved. (For example, a decrease in volume alcohol intake can be achieved via a range of methods, including immediate cessation of drinking;

gradual weekly reduction in units: 50–40–30–20; stepwise unit reduction: 50–25–12–6.) The client will also need to make a decision about by when the plan will be realized; such a decision will help the individual to build in a timescale for change. Counsellors should be prepared to ask clients directly about timing (e.g. 'About how long do you think you will need to decide about change?' or 'If you decide to take action, when do you see yourself doing this?'). Such questions will help clients to frame their ideas about behaviour change, and may help to 'unfreeze' clients who have become 'stuck' in contemplation. Unrealistic timescales should be pursued with clients who find it difficult to be objective about this fundamental concept (e.g. 'You have previously taken several months to achieve what you are planning to accomplish in a few days; do you think you need to revise your schedule?'). Planning to avoid subsequent **relapse** may thus be included in the stage of contemplation.

Successful transition from contemplation to action requires clients to disengage from their previous attitudes, values, beliefs or behaviours. This may involve detachment from previous ways or means of coping, and/or from people, and/or from places. Clients may, however, have 'unfinished business' which, if left undiscussed, can be a major barrier to a transition into action. (It can also potentiate subsequent relapse.) This unfinished business can take several forms, including talking about 'old' ways; criticizing 'new' ways; sabotaging reform attempts. Counsellors should be prepared to encourage clients to resolve unfinished business during the contemplation stage, to preclude its later re-emergence.

In addition, counsellors should also discuss fully with clients what they think will work and what will not work. Clients should be viewed as 'experts' about their own drinking habits, and should be given credit for previous reform attempts (e.g. 'Previously you managed to stop drinking for six weeks; maybe it won't be as difficult as you think to do it again this time'). Counsellors can give periodic progress reports during the stage of contemplation, to provide feedback about the transition towards eventual action.

Ways to avoid dehumanizing clients

1 The counsellor should avoid naive, single-level solutions, which over-simplify complex problems. Alcohol problems involve many variables connected to time, place, people and situations; the complex template of drinking will require a sophisticated behaviour analysis.
2 The counsellor should avoid 'blaming the victim'; drinkers are

often victims of their own circumstances, and require sensitive management.

3 Counselling should not proceed using inadequate information, or from the perpetuation of myths about the client (e.g. 'This person will never change'). The counsellor should establish a sound information base.

4 The counsellor should not risk non-involvement of clients in their change attempts. The counsellor should adopt a multi-level approach and work with clients on several aspects of their problems if necessary.

5 Counselling should not be based on promises, but results. The counsellor should work with clarity via a focus on detail and specifics.

6 'Learned helplessness' (or over-dependence) in clients should be actively discouraged.

7 'False individualism' should be avoided; clients should be considered in the context of the environment which supports their drinking patterns.

8 Counselling should be aimed at the roots of the problem, rather than at surface aspects.

9 The counsellor should build in an examination of the cultural dimensions of the client's drinking, and its personal meaning.

Evaluation

Skilled counsellors will not only aim for proficiency with techniques and procedures, but also be interested in evaluation. While evaluation in this field has been notoriously difficult to achieve, even novice counsellors should integrate measurement into their personal approach. Such measurement attempts focus on an evaluation of the process of counselling (i.e. what happens along the way) or on the outcome (i.e. what happens afterwards). While process and outcome evaluation are equally important, there are barriers to doing both. Counsellors will have to work hard to commit themselves to an area which has been frequently neglected. Skilled counsellors do not separate their counselling practice from an evaluation of its effects.

Acknowledgements

The author wishes to acknowledge the help of Bryan Masterson, Jane Finlay and Wendy Janvrin-Tipping.

References

Baldwin, S., Wilson, M., Lancaster, A. and Allsop, D. (1988) *Ending Offending: An Alcohol Training Resources Pack for Work with Young Offenders*, Glasgow: Scottish Council on Alcohol.

DiClemente, C.C. and Prochaska, J.O. (1982) 'Self-change and therapy change of smoking behavior: a comparison of processes of change of cessation and maintenance', *Addictive Behaviors* 7: 133–42.

McMurran, M. (1987) *There's No Booze Behind Bars*, HMYOI Glen Parva, London: HMSO.

Miller, W.R. (1983) 'Motivational interviewing with problem drinkers', *Behavioural Psychotherapy* 11: 147–72.

Miller, W.R., Sovereign, R.G. and Krege, B. (1987) 'Motivational interviewing with problem drinkers: II The Drinkers' Check-Up as a preventative intervention', *Behavioural Psychotherapy* 16: 251–68.

Prochaska, J.O. (1979) *Systems of Psychotherapy: A Transtheoretical Perspective*, Homewood, Ill: Dorsey Press.

Prochaska, J.O. and DiClemente, C.C. (1982) 'Transtheoretical therapy: towards a more integrative model of change', *Psychotherapy Theory, Research and Practice*, 19, 3: 276–88.

—— (1983) 'Stages and processes of self-change of smoking: toward an integrative model of change', *Journal of Consulting and Clinical Psychology* 51: 390–5.

—— (1986) 'Towards a comprehensive model of change', in W.R. Miller and N. Heather (eds) *Treating Addictive Behaviors: Processes of Change*, New York: Plenum Press.

Robertson, I. and Heather, N. (1985) *So You Want to Cut Down Your Drinking*, Edinburgh: Scottish Health Education Group.

Chapter four

Helping those who want to change

Duncan Raistrick

What is the action stage?

When clients present to treatment agencies, counsellors are often tempted to presume them to be at the action stage; interventions appropriate to the action stage are perhaps those that are most developed and most attractive. Two possible consequences flow from this: either clients are selected for treatment because they are indeed at the action stage (sometimes referred to as 'motivated') and the outcome from treatment will then be generally good. Alternatively clients are given inappropriate treatment because they are incorrectly assumed to be at the action stage, in which case the outcome will generally be poor. The key feature of the action stage is the emergence of a good-quality decision to make change. The emphasis here is on the firmness and the depth of decision; it is commonplace for everyone to make resolutions about changing undesirable behaviours, for example at New Year, but the resolve is rarely sustained. The determination to change a behaviour, such as drinking, which probably has many benefits as well as some problems, will sometimes be generated quite suddenly, perhaps in response to an adverse life event, but more usually it has to be carefully cultivated by the counsellor over a lengthy period. The counsellor should be circumspect about the quality of a decision to change which is presented in the setting of a person feeling unwell as the result of a 'binge'.

The action stage is marked by a firm decision or commitment to change. Clients will make statements such as 'I want to cut down on my drinking', 'My drinking is causing too many problems for me', or 'I am much more sure this time that I want to give up drink altogether'. The commitment to change need not necessarily be to do with the drinking but may be concerned with a different level. For example a client might say, 'Drinking won't be a problem if I can control my panic attacks'. In this example the counsellor must

58

make a judgement about the relationship between the panic attacks and the drinking and whether or not controlling the anxiety will actually affect the drinking. Another example might be, 'I can't change my drinking until I get out of this house'. Again there is an indication of commitment to change, but in this example it is living circumstances; this is a social level change, and again begs the question of whether improvement in drinking behaviour will passively follow rehousing. As well as presenting to specialist agencies, people in the action stage often approach the general practitioner. Accordingly this chapter includes some information on withdrawal drug regimes and the use of alcohol sensitizing agents. The emphasis is, however, on cognitive and behavioural interventions which can be used over a range of settings.

Case study   Being in the action stage

Jayne is a 28-year-old social worker who had reached the action stage when she first came to a specialist alcohol treatment service. She saw her family as having prejudiced and self-interested value systems which she felt to be in conflict with since she went to university to read English. She had fostered a self-image around what she described as 'socialist', 'permissive' thinking; her interests were mainly with the arts and in particular an active role in a politically orientated theatre group. She lived with another woman who wanted a sexual relationship with her and this had been a long-term stress as Jayne felt 'asexual'. They lived in the student quarter.

Jayne had experimented with a few drugs at university and still smoked cannabis, but was happy with her use of this substance. Her drinking career also took off at university and, more or less since qualifying, it had been her habit to go to the pub most nights of the week; her concern at initial contact was that she had started to drink at lunchtimes and recognized that it was only a matter of time before this would adversely affect her work, which she very much enjoyed. She had decided to try and give up alcohol completely.

A plan to try for total abstinence instantly failed. Two things had gone wrong: first the social importance of evening drinking had been under-estimated and Jayne's wish for a psychotherapeutic approach had been ignored. This was a care plan failure: Jayne remained in the action stage. A new plan set reasonable limits and self-monitoring of evening drinking only and built in time for work at a different level, namely the relationship, allowing more free expression for Jayne to resolve that conflict in her own way. The important first task for the counsellor, however, was to gain control on the drinking.

Objectives

Once clients have reached the action stage then the job of the counsellor is to bring the drinking into line with their new thoughts about themselves. Say the new thinking is 'I see myself as a social drinker' then there will be certain techniques appropriate to moving the client from excessive to social drinking; similarly if the client's new thinking is 'I see myself as a non-drinker' then it may be that different techniques would be applied to achieve total abstinence (interventions at levels other than substance misuse are considered in other chapters). Failure to achieve drinking goals does not necessarily imply relapse: the crucial factor is the client's commitment to change, not change itself. A misjudged treatment plan may account for lack of progress just as much as clients' failure to maintain their resolution.

Assessment

In order to get the treatment plan right the counsellor has to decide how much treatment is required? How should the treatment be given? The plan should be informed by an appreciation of the client's intake, dependence, related problems and expectations.

Intake

This fundamental measure is actually very difficult to capture in a simple, summary form. It is customary to estimate intake either by units or by grams of alcohol. The counsellor must strike a balance between the usefulness of the information and the time taken to collect it. Something akin to a bracketing approach may be adequate: how long since last drink? How many days drinking that week? How much on the heaviest day? Is this typical of the last six months? Asking about the heaviest day gives license to report high levels of intake, which will not only reflect more general use but also correlate with dependence and alcohol-related harm (Davidson and Raistrick 1986). A pattern of intake characterized by episodes of severe intoxication may demand a different treatment plan, likely to be associated with different kinds of alcohol-related problems, compared to a pattern characterized by regular heavy intake. In broad brush terms the episodes of intoxication pattern of drinking suggests treatment strategies based on avoidance of high-risk situations and people, whereas regular heavy intake suggests strategies aimed at reducing dependence, or, in other words, unlearning a drinking habit that has become enmeshed in everyday life.

Dependence

Both the concept and significance of dependence remain controversial (Edwards 1986). The view of dependence taken here is of a psychological state, which can therefore be measured only by indirect markers; in practical terms it is an indication of how difficult change will be. A high level of treatment involvement is associated with good outcome in high dependence clients while the reverse is true for low dependence. A brief clinical enquiry should establish stereotyping of drinking pattern; salience of drinking; and drinking in anticipation of or in response to withdrawal symptoms. There are a number of self-completion scales available for the measurement of dependence.

Alcohol-related harm

A checklist, either on paper or in the head, covering the many aspects of alcohol-related harm will help the counsellor see at a glance the range and severity of problems to be dealt with. In a medical setting the blood tests serum glutamic oxalacetic transaminase (SGOT), gamma gutamyl transpeptidase (GGT), mean corpuscular volume (MCV) and high density lipoprotein (HDL) are useful measures of alcohol intake and tissue damage. What is a problem is to a large extent idiosyncratic but all aspects of harm that are identified by the client as a problem should be kept in high profile in order to help sustain the motivation to change. The counsellor must also be alert for harm that requires treatment irrespective of whether the client sees a problem, for example child neglect, poor nutrition, accidental self-injury, mixing alcohol and medication, or non-payment of essential bills.

Self-efficacy and behavioural skills

If the client is to negotiate the action stage successfully then a certain amount of preparation work will probably need to be done. Clients are at a very vulnerable point here: they have handed over their defence mechanisms, probably feel guilty and probably feel low in self-esteem. A failure or setback at this point could be disastrous and the counsellor has the critical task of setting achievable goals and ensuring adequate support to pursue them or else risk losing the client from the action stage. The most important predictor of successful behaviour change is confidence, or to use the jargon **self-efficacy**; confidence alone is insufficient and to be helpful must be tied into behavioural skills. A brief clinical enquiry should establish what are the expectations of the client; how long goals are believed to be sustainable; whether there is an understanding of and willingness to use behavioural techniques.

In some circumstances clients may enter the action stage carried there by a change in drinking behaviour, perhaps enforced by illness or incarceration. If their thoughts about themselves come to match the new drinking pattern then they may move quickly into maintenance (see Chapter 5). In any event the principles of interventions in the action stage remain the same.

Therapeutic interventions

The addiction field has, on the face of it, an inexplicable passion to indulge in self-flagellation, crying either that 'treatment doesn't work' or 'if anything works we don't know what it is'. However, anyone who takes a look through the research literature will be cheered to find neither of these viewpoints to be true, although outcome studies will always include caveats and call for more research (Miller 1986). The self-flagellators may be picking up on the fact that people sometimes move out of problem drinking without the help of professionals or specialist alcohol counsellors. There may also be a hidden agenda which conceals a reluctance by counsellors to reject or refine interventions not shown to be effective, but, worse, a failure more enthusiastically to embrace interventions that *have* been shown to work. Table 4.1. summarizes the minimal and extended interventions described in this chapter. It is curious, and in some ways worrying, that popular and commonly applied interventions targeted at the action stage, such as traditional psychotherapy, confrontation and unstructured counselling, have no established efficacy. It is equally curious that inexperienced staff are often put into a front-line treatment role when careful research suggests that this may be damaging to the client (Sanchez-Craig 1987). The great paradox of alcohol treatment is that while the condition has a generally good outlook and 'spontaneous' recovery is common, there is an excess mortality rate among heavy drinkers which places a great responsibility upon counsellors for the overall care of their clients.

Table 4.1 Interventions

Minimal interventions

Self-help manuals
Advice only
Assessment and feedback

- intake
- dependence
- related problems
- self-efficacy

Extended interventions

Detoxification
- out-patient/community
- in-patient

Problem-solving approach
- problem definition
- self-monitoring
- brainstorming
- verification
- rewards

Changing expectations
- alcohol-sensitizing agents
- aversion therapies
- cue exposure

Community reinforcement

Minimal interventions

Exactly what constitutes a **minimal intervention** has not been defined: the phrase has come to be used to refer to a range of treatments that are economical with staff time, meaning no more input than two sessions and often even less. Apart from the time issue minimal interventions have the advantages of being adaptable to different settings, for example the home, the general medical ward, the prison or the office, and can readily be used by different professional groups. Minimal interventions are seen as most appropriate for individuals with low or middle dependence scores and few alcohol-related problems, but this should not be taken to imply that they will be totally ineffective with other groups (Heather 1989).

Self-help manuals

At one end of the spectrum of minimal interventions are self-help manuals. The self-help manual can be sent out by post or bought commercially and therefore be completely anonymous, or it can be used as an adjunct to counselling. Typically manuals stress that they are not for 'alcoholics' and try to avoid any stigma that might be associated with labelling problems, in short they are for you and me. Self-help manuals have differed from simple education leaflets or booklets in that they additionally contain a systematic approach to changing drinking behaviour through self-monitoring, functional analysis, goal-setting and relapse-prevention techniques usually presented in a format that is culture-friendly. Evaluation of such therapeutic tools is enormously difficult; none the less there is evidence that the manuals perform significantly better than educational handouts alone. In one six-months follow-up, manual users were reported as reducing intake by 40 per cent compared to 25 per cent by an educational leaflet group; furthermore the manual users showed greater improvement in various areas of physical and social well-being (Heather *et al.* 1986). Clearly there is a case for making self-help manuals very easily available, but in reality they are not sufficiently accessible.

Advice only

It has generally been found that where extended treatment is compared with a shorter treatment there are few differences, although, of course, there are caveats and limits to the rule. Inspired by these findings a number of researchers have created and evaluated so-called 'advice only' packages, which have similar advantages to the self-help manuals but have the additional ambition of making an assessment of an individual's drinking and drink-related problems, and feeding back this information to be digested and acted upon in whatever way the client then chooses.

One example of an advice only package, the *Drinkers' Check-Up*, (Miller *et al.* 1988), uses an intensive two-hour assessment package, which includes psychological and medical examination, and two weeks later a follow-up, feedback session; this approach has achieved a reduction of 20 per cent in weekly consumption and 37 per cent in peak intoxication levels. It could be argued that the *Drinkers' Check-Up* is actually rather hungry on resource and only appropriate to a specialist clinic, which begs the question 'How little advice is effective?' The answer, not very helpfully, is that there is no answer: it depends. Variants of advice only packages are being evaluated in different settings, including general practice and general medical wards, with encouraging results. The ingredients that seem to be important are delivery of the advice by an experienced and authoritative counsellor, an objective assessment of alcohol-related problems, an empathic quality of intervention, feedback to highlight discrepancies between desired goal and present state, clear direction given to achieve the desired goal, and one follow up session. The initial advice interview is likely to last 30–60 minutes.

The exciting message from the work that has been done so far on understanding the properties and performance of minimal intervention is that they can be used by all therapists, specialist or non-specialist, experienced or inexperienced, and can be modified for use in any setting to achieve any desired drinking goal. In numerical terms it will be these kinds of interventions that have the greatest impact on drinking problems in the population as a whole.

As a footnote to this section careful note should be made of the range of self-help organizations for problem drinkers, of which Alcoholics Anonymous (AA) is undoubtedly the best known. Commitment to attending AA meetings may be far from a minimal intervention, indeed it may be an 'alternative addiction'; however, from the counsellor's point of view, the need to provide intensive support may be obviated by this self-help community.

Extended interventions

For clients with high dependence scores and multiple problem areas then more intensive, possibly specialist treatment is indicated. For these individuals the action stage usually means achieving an alcohol-free state as a prelude to further treatment, which may then embrace either a controlled drinking goal or a total abstinence goal. Of course the treatment plan will not normally be restricted to a consideration of the substance misuse.

Detoxification

'Drying out' or detoxification is an intervention most appropriate to the action stage, but sometimes undertaken as an expedience at other stages of change. It can be defined as the process of rapidly achieving an alcohol-free state: the aim is to achieve this agreed objective with the minimum of discomfort to the client and at the same time monitoring for co-existing problems in order to ensure maximum safety. If there are objective signs of withrawal symptoms it is usual to prescribe a tranquillizer to attenuate the severity of the symptoms. For more than 90 per cent of cases alcohol withdrawal will be uneventful and uncomplicated. Professionals must, therefore, overcome the dangers of complacency and be vigilant for co-existing conditions which may be immediately detectable, for example head injury, drug overdose or chest infection. Some co-existing conditions become apparent only as the detoxification proceeds, for example depression or obsessional neurosis. It is

Table 4.2 Alcohol withdrawal

Tremulous state (peak 4–12 hours)
Shaking of hands
Tremulous face and body
Retching and vomiting
Sweating
Increased pulse rate
Anxiety
Dysphoria
Irritability

Tremulous-hallucinatory state (peak 4–12 hours)
In addition to above:
Illusions
Fleeting hallucinations

Seizures (peak 36 hours)

Alcoholic delirium (peak 72 hours)
Marked over-arousal
Visual hallucinations
Delusions

---

useful to have a standardized method of recording and monitoring the severity of symptoms throughout a detoxification programme (see Table 4.2).

Alcohol withdrawal symptoms will occur only in people who have become tolerant to the effects of drinking: an abrupt cessation or marked reduction of their intake may then precipitate withdrawal symptoms. From the medical point of view detoxification can generally be managed on an out-patient basis covering, if necessary, the withdrawal with a long-acting benzodiazepine such as chlordiazepoxide (in doses up to 200mg daily but more typically starting at perhaps 80mg daily). If there are signs of perceptual disturbance or a history of seizures or alcoholic delirium then in-patient care is prudent.

Problem-solving approach

A problem-solving or behavioural self-management approach is an infinitely flexible way to move forward with someone who has completed detoxification or alternatively someone who continues to drink but has some control over consumption and is none the less in the action stage (Goldfried and Goldfried 1980). In the drinking context the approach can be used to try for either controlled or total abstinence goals, but, of course, need not be restricted to drinking as the problem behaviour. It can be applied on a one-to-one basis or in a group context. Counsellors will have their own idiosyncrasies but in general the following headings should serve to guide:

Problem definition   The first step is to draw up a hierarchy of specific problems: 'drinking too much' is not specific but 'drinking more than five pints on Friday night' would be a good enough definition. Having drawn up a list decide what the pay-offs are for each problem behaviour defined: the pay-offs might be entirely related to nice things, such as meeting friends, or might be to do with avoiding unpleasant things, such as feeling low in mood. The important principle is that clients choose the most important problems for themselves and are guided by the counsellor only in respect of the precision of definitions. In jargon this is a behavioural analysis.

Self-monitoring   Having identified the target behaviour, in this case drinking, then it is useful to check out if the initial assumptions are correct. A drinking diary records date and time of drinking occasions, place, who with and accompanying mood or thoughts. Monitoring will in itself probably change the target behaviour. Even if detoxification and abstinence have been achieved, monitoring 'craving' for a drink may be useful. Self-monitoring is, however, generally more applicable to those in the contemplation stage.

Brainstorming   The next step is to work on a plan to change the target behaviour. The plan must specify the limits of change, the timescale, the consequences and the method: in short the outcome must be verifiable. The plan is restrained only by the imagination and skills of the counsellor and client; it will always be entertaining and usually productive to 'brainstorm' and generate a list of options to consider, however crazy they may seem. The counsellor must take care that the final plan is achievable and that the resources required, for example time from the counsellor, support from a spouse, scope to manipulate environmental factors, are all available.

The self-monitoring exercise will have identified high-risk situations and where possible these should be avoided until such time as the counsellor believes that the client is appropriately confident to deal with the risk. Confidence can be built up in several ways: the use of role-play, imagining difficult situations and planning a response, such as refusing drinks, and suggesting tricks for sticking to agreed limits, for example start and finish with non-alcoholic drinks, have only long drinks and sip at a predetermined rate.

There are no absolute rules for setting limits. It is convenient to work in units or standard drinks (half-pint of beer = glass of wine = single spirit) and ideally the weekly consumption should fall within the recommended 'safe limits' as published by the Health Education Authority. Initially this may be unrealistic and considerable judgement will be required with an individual care plan. The general public, however, has not taken to the idea of units.

Verification If in doubt about any treatment plan then the risk of misadventure is minimized by an early review to see if targets have been met. Any failure to achieve goals should be attributed to a flawed plan, not a failure of the client; a new, more realistic plan should be devised and the process repeated.

Reward As behaviour change occurs then it is important to build in a variety of rewards. For the first one or two weeks of change, rewards tend to be spontaneous, for example compliments from others, feeling better, finances improved; to move on into the maintenance stage there is a need to find new interests and define new values that are incompatible with a return to the old behaviour.

Changing expectations

However much family, friends or professionals may see a drinking *problem*, for the individual drinking is usually functional or desirable in some way: it may simply be that being intoxicated is a fun experience, or it may be that drinking makes unpleasant things (e.g. deprived living circumstances, relationship difficulties, withdrawal symptoms) seem, at least in the short term, more tolerable. Alcohol is an extremely versatile drug and can be palliative or recreational in many disparate situations. A number of therapies have the same general aim, namely to change the expectation of a good effect, be that palliative or recreational, to the expectation of a bad effect from drinking. This approach is really suitable only for an abstinence goal.

The simplest and most widely used treatment of this genre is disulfiram (Antabuse), which is one of several so-called **alcohol-sensitizing agents**. Disulfiram is a drug which has no observable effect unless alcohol is also consumed, in which case the normal breakdown of alcohol is blocked and there is an accumulation of the toxic chemical, acetaldelyde. Acetaldelyde has the effect of causing nausea, vomiting, flushing and palpitations. The effective dose of disulfiram is unpredictable and often exceeds the standard regimen of one tablet daily; it is useful to give a test dose of alcohol (say the equivalent of two pints of beer) to clients taking disulfiram to confirm the disulfiram-ethanol reaction (this alcohol challenge is not intended to produce an unduly unpleasant effect). It is important to achieve an effective dose level because clients will often test out whether or not they can drink on top of disulfiram. The pharmacological effectiveness of disulfiram persists for two to three days after the drug is discontinued and therefore offers good protection against the impulsive or ill-considered decision to drink. Disulfiram should be used with caution in patients who have cardiovascular disease, and is contra-indicated in pregnancy and clients with a history of psychosis. Even without selecting subjects in the action stage the results of disulfiram therapy are impressive. Over a twelve-month period clients on disulfiram have been found to have half as many drinking days as those taking no disulfiram or an ineffective dose (Fuller *et al.* 1986). Disulfiram would normally be seen as an adjunct to counselling and would be discontinued once the client was well established in the maintenance stage.

A number of techniques, collectively known as **aversion therapies**, have the same objective of altering expectations about drinking; like disulfiram, they have been extensively researched and found to be effective at changing drinking behaviour. The general principle is to pair an unpleasant experience with alcohol consumption. This approach fell into disrepute because the pioneering works used excessively harsh noxious experiences, such as induced apnoea and electric shock. A much more acceptable technique called **covert sensitization** works on the basis of pairing in imagination a favourite drinking scene with something unpleasant, such as feeling nauseous; the effectiveness depends upon the extent to which a nausea-inducing scene produces some physiological response. The technique is limited by requiring considerable expertise and time, but, none the less, is a useful alternative to disulfiram and similar pharmacological methods.

Alcohol-sensitizing agents and aversion techniques have a place where the aim is simply to prevent drinking in any circumstances. A rather more refined treatment, **cue exposure**, may be useful where one particular cue or trigger dominates those occasions where drinking is out of control or is in some way problematic. An example of such a trigger might be blood alcohol level as manifest in the belief that two whiskies inevitably means finishing a bottle. The principle here is to expose individuals to the particular trigger (in this case a blood alcohol level equivalent to drinking two whiskies) and then allow clients, under supervision, to consume as much additional whisky as they wish while encouraging them to resist drinking anything at all. After successfully resisting the trigger on a number of occasions then the beliefs and expectations associated with drinking two whiskies are changed. Again this is an intervention requiring time and some expertise. Only one example of the general principle has been described.

Community reinforcement approach

However important it might be to unravel the complexities of a particular drinking behaviour it remains the case that drinking takes place in the social context of the real world. This rather obvious fact has been exploited in a particularly elegant programme in the USA known as the community reinforcement approach (Sisson and Azrin 1989). The programme is abstinence orientated and participants all receive disulfiram (Antabuse) taken under carefully prepared conditions supervised by their spouse or a significant other; in return for abstinence the programme offers counselling aimed at improving happiness within the relationship, a job club, social and recreational counselling and dealing with difficult drink-related situations. At six-month follow-up clients receiving disulfiram and supportive counselling reported over 50 per cent drinking days compared to virtually no drinking for individuals in the community reinforcement programme, who also did better in terms of employment and time spent at home. The programme also has some useful ideas for helping the more isolated and possibly more damaged drinker.

Case study   Community reinforcement approach
***

Derek is a 46-year-old single, unemployed man, who was admitted into a general medical ward after being brought up to Accident and Emergency by the police; he had an empty tablet bottle labelled Hemineverin (a tranquillizer) and there was concern that he might have taken an overdose of this drug in combination with alcohol. In the event he was quickly detoxified and made an uneventful recovery. Derek gave a history of alcohol misuse dating back to when he was in the army. He had lost most of his jobs because of drinking; his wife, with their two children, separated from him three years previously. He was now homeless.

Derek told the nurses on the ward, 'I don't want to drink – I don't like it'. The ward staff were not generally enthusiastic about looking after problem drinkers but recognized that Derek was deteriorating both physically and mentally, and was also expressing the wish to give up drink. The problem here was that Derek had always used alcohol both to enjoy himself and to cope with life's problems: he had the expectation that alcohol would always have a good effect and knew of few other activities that were rewarding. In the short term the balance was all in favour of drinking.

A plan was set up using the principles of the community reinforcement approach. In return for abstinence the staff would arrange a place in a 'dry house' which was supported by a social worker who encouraged the residents to feel involved in the upkeep of the house; a promise was also made, if all went well, to help in making a reconciliation with his wife. The dry-house place would not be available for two weeks, which meant an interim stay at the Crypt. Derek himself was reasonably sure that with day support, the help of a prescription for disulfiram (supervised), and the promises made to sort out his main concerns he would want to remain abstinent in order to achieve the longer-term goals.

Conclusion

Wishful thinking, both by the counsellor and the client, will sometimes lead to an incorrect assessment that a person has reached the action stage. As seen in Chapters 2 and 3 there is plenty of scope for intervention in pre-contemplation or in the contemplation stage: indeed a prolonged period of motivational work may well be necessary before the action stage is truly reached. In some ways the simplest and most rewarding work is with clients at the action stage; however, the most important objective is to give the right treatment at the right time. When clients have reached the action stage they may require surprisingly little help from counsellors and 'treatment' needs to be dispensed with due restraint.

References

Davidson, R. and Raistrick, D.S. (1986) 'The validity of the Short Alcohol Dependence Data (SADD) questionnaire: a short self-report questionnaire for the assessment of alcohol dependence', *British Journal of Addiction* 81: 217–22.

Edwards, G. (1986) 'The alcohol dependence syndrome: a concept as stimulus to enquiry', *British Journal of Addiction* 81: 533–45.

Fuller, R.K., Branchey, L., Brightwell, D.R., Derman, R.M., Emrick, C.D., Iber, F.C., James, K.E., Lacoursiere, R.B., Lee, K.K., Loweritam, I., Maany, I., Neiderheiser, D., Nocks, J.J. and Shaw, S. (1986) 'Disulfiram treatment of alcoholism: a Veterans Administration co-operative study', *Journal of Mental and Nervous Diseases* 256: 1,449–55.

Goldfried, M.R. and Goldfried, A.P. (1980) 'Cognitive change methods', in H.K., Kanfer and A.P. Goldstein (eds) *Helping People Change*, Oxford: Pergamon.

Duncan Raistrick

Heather, N. (1989) 'Brief intervention strategies', in R.K. Hester and W.R. Miller (eds) *Handbook of Alcoholism Treatment Approaches: Effective Approaches*, Oxford: Pergamon.

Heather, N., Whitton, B. and Robertson, I. (1986) 'Evaluation of a self-help manual for media-recruited problem drinkers: six month follow-up results', *British Journal of Clinical Psychology* 25: 19–34.

Miller, W.R. (1986) 'The effectiveness of alcoholism treatment: what research reveals', in W.R. Miller and N. Heather (eds) *Treating Addictive Behaviour*, New York: Plenum Press.

Miller, W.R., Sovereign, R.G. and Krege, B. (1988) 'Motivational interviewing with problem drinkers: II the drinkers' check-up as a preventive intervention', *Behavioural Psychotherapy* 16: 251–68.

Sanchez-Craig, M. (1987) 'Short-term treatment: conceptual and practical issues', *Fourth International Conference on the Treatment of Addictive Behaviours*, Norway.

Sisson, R. and Azrin, N. (1989) 'The community reinforcement approach', in R.K. Hester and W.R. Miller (eds) *Handbook of Alcoholism Treatment Approaches*, Oxford: Pergamon.

Chapter five

Helping those who relapse

Bill Saunders and Steven Allsop

Introduction

Models are aids to understanding and while usually being scaled
down or simplified versions of the real thing, a good model will
allow some appreciation of the intricacies of reality to be ascer-
tained. A further test of a model is to ask just how was the subject
matter understood before the current model was derived? With
regard to Prochaska and DiClemente's stages of change model
(1986), it is difficult, nearly a decade on, to recall how we used to
make sense of many complex things. Such difficult and diverse
issues as prognosis, 'motivation', the role of counselling in addiction
behaviours, treatment failure and the giving up process were often
considered in isolation. As outlined in Chapter 1, the advantage of
Prochaska and DiClemente's work is that such debates can now be
structured within the organizing principle of pre-contemplator –
contemplator – actioner (changer) – maintainer.

Perhaps, however, the single greatest strength of the stages of
change model is that it intuitively appeals and makes good sense.
Within its framework people can identify and comprehend their
own troublesome behaviours. What also distinguishes the stages of
change model is that in a much conflicted and confused field the
model is readily accepted. The overwhelming response when teaching about the model is that it is useful, and has an application
beyond the relatively narrow enclave of addiction behaviour. It also
appears to be non-denominational, appealing to disease and social-
learning adherents alike. It is in fact one of those few topics in the
addiction field that can be taught and discussed without fear of
antagonizing ideological sensitivities. It is a good day when 'Prochaska and DiClemente' are on the teaching syllabus.

What is maintenance and relapse?

Having noted all the above and with the perspective that the stages of change model is a valuable 'cognitive-map' for any clinician or researcher to adopt, it has to be noted that specific consideration of relapse, in a book predicated on the stages of change model, is somewhat misplaced. The essential reason for this is simple. Relapse is not a stage in the process of change. However, there is some confusion here. In Prochaska and DiClemente's authoritative outline of their model (1986), relapse does appear in what is entitled a 'revolving-door' model of the stages of change and is included at the expense of 'pre-contemplation'. To say (as Prochaska and DiClemente do) that 'a major problem in the treatment of addiction behaviour is that most individuals do not progress linearly through the stages of change' and that 'relapse is the rule rather than the exception', does not, irrespective of the validity of these statements, give 'relapse' the status of being a stage. Relapse is in fact the vehicle whereby individuals travel back to other previous stages. Further, it must also be noted that 'maintainers' are by definition 'maintainers' because they do not relapse; thus the very factors which encourage maintenance are also those that prevent relapse. Again 'relapse' is a process or event that can plunge maintainers back into the earlier stages of the model; but it is not of itself a stage.

None the less the stages of change model is very valuable in helping us come to grips with the complexities of relapse, and this contention is substantiated below. First, however, it is useful, in relation to relapse, to stress an important and clinically valuable aspect of the stages of change model. While movement, via relapse, back to contemplation may be a common occurrence, the model allows relapsers to go straight back into action or presumably to revert totally to the pre-contemplation stage. Thus a 'relapse' can be a transient event for an actioner or changer without automatically being debilitating. Clinicians do perhaps need to be reminded of this.

Second, Prochaska and DiClemente also note from their smoking research that 'the average self-changer made three serious revolutions through the stages of change before they exit', that is became change maintainers. We consider this an important statement that merits greater emphasis, and indeed we consider that the long-term value of 'relapse', or movement up and down the stages of change, is poorly represented by the Prochaska and DiClemente's revolving door diagram. Our emphasis would be that people who have attempted an action and who have been successful for a while, but who then revert to their old ways, need to be distinguished from those contemplators who have yet to take action. As a number of researchers have shown, knowledge that you have coping skills that do work is a better predictor of good outcome than is the absolute number of coping skills you may possess. Thus people learn how not to relapse by putting their skills to the test. While they may eventually fall back, the experience of how you survived for a while is meaningful for the next attempt. Such learning and value needs to be articulated and what we would like to see incorporated into the revolving door model of Prochaska and DiClemente is a sense of 'spiralling-out' rather than going around and around (see Figure 5.1). This may reflect better the realities of the relapse process and its relationship to eventual permanent behaviour change. To emphasize this further it is useful to cite Lichenstein and Weiss, who noted that people who attempted to quit smoking but failed, as opposed to those who had yet to embark on change,

> Show important increases in self-efficacy, decreases in temptation to smoke, and increases in the use of particular change processes such as helping relationships. Positive gains occur even though those individuals return to regular smoking.
>
> (Lichenstein and Weiss 1986)

Such gains are perhaps better suggested as a spiral rather than a revolving vortex. The caveat here, however, must be that often repeated experiences of failure can be only detrimental to confidence. So it is a matter of learning from a few relapses rather than being overwhelmed by the experience of many.

An additional and neglected aspect of relapse is also highlighted by an examination of relapse and the stages of change model. As has been well demonstrated by Marlatt and Gordon (1980) and also Annis (1986), the causes of relapse can be variously attributed. Clients who have relapses seem to be vulnerable to different situational determinants. While some may succumb to social situations or strong desires to drink, others will give up their attempts to change because of unpleasant mood states or interpersonal difficulties. While this classification of relapse has obvious clinical implications, the Prochaska and DiClemente model also suggests that a longitudinal view is necessary. It is possible that people relapse for different reasons because of where they are located in the stages of change. Thus people who relapse as 'early-actioners' may do so for different reasons from those who are maintainers. Unfortunately in the classification of relapse work that

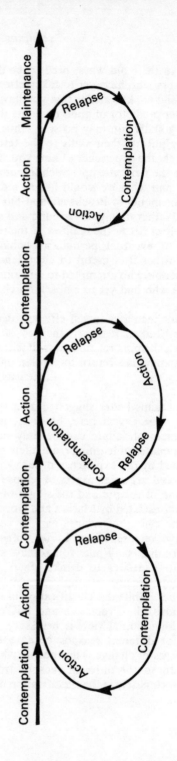

Figure 5.1 A spiralling-out model of change

has been reported, this temporal feature has been ignored. Although writing in a different context, Edwards has hinted at this failure to see relapse as a process that can occur at anytime in the change cycle. He noted

> the phrase relapse prevention may usefully stimulate thought, break old moulds, get the adrenalin flowing, give the title to a book, but at the end of the day it can be an invitation to an artificial segmentation of the interacting, total and fluctuating process of change.
>
> (Edwards 1987)

What is being stressed by Edwards is that relapse, or the potential for going back on one's vows to change, can occur at any stage, and that singling out relapse for investigation requires an appreciation that factors involved in the pre-contemplator, contemplator, actioner (changer) and maintainer stages can, and do, influence one's relapse potential.

This can be well demonstrated by reference to some of the catalysts or processes of change that have been identified as underpinning the Prochaska and DiClemente model and which have been summarized in Chapter 1. What is clear from such examination is that investigators of relapse would do well to attend to the impact of the different processes of change as variables within any relapse model. Attention to these processes makes one more alert to the impact of the passing of time, and the events of life that accompany that passage, upon people's resolutions to change. Interestingly, while relapse work has not been directly based on the Prochaska and DiClemente processes of change, all of the processes have been implicated in relapse studies. Each process will now be considered and examples of directly relevant relapse research given. It is perhaps necessary to stress that, rather than being discrete entities, the various processes do overlap. Thus while the stages of change are presented as a linear model it is clear from the writings of Prochaska and DiClemente that the processes involved do merge into one another, or perhaps more accurately, can occur simultaneously.

Change processes as applied to relapse

Process	Description	Impact on relapse proneness*
1 Consciousness-raising	The individual becomes aware of,	The quality of the initial resolution to

77

	and/or seeks out information and knowledge about the behaviour. Becomes sensitive to the issues and may discuss with credible sources or professionals. Begins to examine own behaviour.	change is important. Robust resolutions do last longer. There is some evidence that strength of intent is predictive of outcome. Consciousness-raising is also consistent with notions of good decision-making.
2 Catharis	Described by Prochaska and DiClemente (1986) as a 'corrective emotional experience', the individual either gradually appreciates the toll of costs relating to the behaviour, or may have a 'road to Damascus' experience. Personal humiliation, acute adverse consequences or narrow escape from disaster may prompt awareness of the need for change.	While poorly understood in psychological terms, the drug literature is replete with examples of 'spontaneous remission' being engendered by a traumatic event. This has been termed a 'critical perceptual shift' and it has also been demonstrated that individuals who can recall adverse consequences and have an apprehension about re-experiencing such situations have higher survival rates.
3 Self-evaluation	AA members talk about the need to do 'a fearless, personal, moral inventory' which is akin to this process of taking stock, and considering one's options.	Recognition of the costs of behaviour plus outcome expectancies – appreciating that a change in behaviour may result in rewards to the individual – have been found to be important in

	'Do I really want to continue like this?' or 'Will I like myself better if I change?' are part of this process.	predicting behaviour. Using Subjective Expected Utility theory (SEU) Sutton (1987) found an association between positive SEU scores and successful quitting of smoking. Relapsers were less optimistic about the value of quitting.
4 Self-liberation	An appreciation that change is possible and 'do-able' is gained. Individuals perceive discontinuing use as being a positive event and that they are capable of doing it.	Self-efficacy (self-mastery of a task) has been argued by various authors to be critical in relapse. Individuals who believe in their ability to cope do better. Other researchers have found self-efficacy to be predictive of outcome (Condiotte and Lichenstein 1981).
5 Helping relationships	The basis of this process is that the individual has someone with whom to discuss progress and gain support. This resource may be a neighbour, priest, dark stranger or a 'professional' counsellor.	While the overall impact of counselling for the addiction behaviours remains much debated, specific relapse prevention programmes have been demonstrated as being effective (Chaney *et al.* 1978). Such programmes incorporate aspects of the above-

		noted processes plus individual support.
6 Reinforcement management	The individual needs to gain benefits from undertaking changes which are tangible. Positive pay-offs are necessary for continued adherence to a change behaviour.	In the alcohol literature the best example of successful reinforcement management is the work of Azrin (1976) and colleagues. Making abstinence 'pay' ensures continued adherence to the resolution to abstain.
7 Counter-conditioning	Alternative behaviours that are rewarding are also necessary and are best if such behaviours are antagonistic to drug use (e.g. jogging for just stopped smokers).	The quality of one's post-change life matters much in maintaining the endeavour. Improved familial relationships, more enjoyable work or marital interactions sustain individuals.
8 Stimulus control	There is a need to avoid and/or manage the cues that promote urges to use drugs.	Most relevant example here is cue-exposure and response-prevention techniques (Rankin 1986). Also, Prochaska and DiClemente (1986) have demonstrated how temptation to use nicotine falls over time and that this is associated with increased confidence in coping with challenges.

*Note: The term 'relapse-proneness' is borrowed from work by Shiffman (1986) to indicate that all behaviour changers are on a continuum of risk for giving up their attempt to change. This 'at-riskness' can vary from individual to individual and more importantly for individuals over time.

Case studies Relapsing

That relapses occur at different stages and for different reasons can be highlighted by reference to relapses reported in the literature. One elegant report is from Tam Stewart's autobiographical account of heroin use in Britain. She duly listed the benefits of quitting heroin use:

> Trips to the ballet and the theatre, holidays abroad, buying new clothes and getting a new hairstyle. At the bottom of the list, as if it did not matter as much as the rest came the single statement 'change life'. It stuck out like a sore thumb. It was the crux of the matter. A new hairdo could not outweigh the hunger for smack. The command to change seemed ludicrously grave and quite impossible to carry out. Nevertheless I got on with the cure, motivated like many others primarily by impecunity. I waited impatiently for the moment when I could relapse.
>
> (Stewart 1987)

Another comes from an earlier investigation of relapse in which we were involved. One respondent noted:

> Saturday night at 9 o'clock I went for a carry-out. I went to a hotel and bought a half-bottle and came home with that. I was fed up. From my window I see them going up and down the road to the pub and you know exactly where they are going and I said I'm going for one as well, that's how it happened. Friends and neighbours I saw, it's only a wee village I stay in and you know everybody in it. You can more or less tell what pub they are going to. I thought I've been off it five months, surely I can go for a nice drink.   (Saunders and Allsop 1987)

Perhaps what is evident the above is that there is no single cause and that while there are some frequently cited reasons for relapsing it would be an error to believe that there is such a thing as a typical relapse. In any analysis of relapses the immediate antecedents of a relapse always need to be considered against the quality of the initial resolution to change and the individual's ongoing commitment to change. And the question do relapses happen to people or do people make relapses happen always merits consideration.

Therapeutic interventions

We hope that the above analysis demonstrates that relapse, or 'a change, either temporary or permanent in a resolution to change' (Saunders and Allsop 1987), can occur for multiple reasons and at any stage in the process of change. The implications of this are that relapse-prevention techniques also need to be multi-modal and be directed at different aspects of the change cycle. Thus we have recently proposed a variegated intervention model (Allsop and Saunders 1988).

For the purposes of this section we outline in detail various clinical strategies which we combined to form part of an experimental evaluation of relapse-prevention strategies (Allsop *et al.* forthcoming). While our formulation of these strategies was not directly based on the Prochaska and DiClemente model (1986), it is clear that the various strategies we employed can be subsumed within the stages of change model. It is important to appreciate the fluid and interlocking nature of the processes of change and how specific strategies can address more than one of the processes. Again what is emphasized is the need to work across the spectrum and develop a multi-modal relapse-intervention package. When employing the techniques described below, counsellors will obviously need to adapt the strategies to fit the needs of individual clients, and the circumstances in which they work. We consider however that apsects of all the following strategies are needed to help people minimize their relapse 'proneness'.

Assessing enhancing and resolution to change

After the usual assessment procedures it is valuable to adopt a style of interviewing, described by Miller (1983) as 'motivational interviewing' (see Chapter 3), which can be used to enhance resolution to change and give a sense of what stage of change individual clients are in. Clients' perceptions of the positive consequences of their drug use would be elicited first, with the counsellor summarizing and paraphrasing the client's responses: 'So you're telling me that the good things about your alcohol use are . . . and . . . and . . . . Is there anything else?' This would be followed by elicitation of the client's perceptions of the negative consequences of alcohol use, for example, 'What are some of the not so good things about your drinking?' The counsellor would always encourage the client to be specific: if a client reported 'health' was a problem, the response would be 'In what way?' or 'Could you give me an example of how that's a problem for you?'

The emphasis should be placed on eliciting concern as opposed to a simple extraction of problems. Thus the counsellor could ask: 'Does that concern you?' or 'In what way does that concern you?' We consider this an important distinction. Having a problem is not necessarily the same as being concerned about that problem. For example, marital disharmony is significant only if the client places value on the marital relationship. This procedure also encourages an individual 'owning' of problems. Counsellors should avoid expressing their own value interpretations of problems, leaving clients the responsibility for generating their own inventories of troubles. The counsellor would then summarize the client's report: 'So you're saying you're concerned about your alcohol use because of . . . and . . . and . . . and . . . . Is there anything else?' The same procedure would be applied to concerns for the future if the client were to continue drinking in the same manner. As client's identify their concerns, it can be useful to keep a visual record on a whiteboard. Thus at the end of each section the counsellor can summarize the client's reports and ascertain the accuracy of the record. It is useful if clients can keep a note of their concerns in a personal notebook which can be used as a record of the programme. The counsellor would acknowledge the client's situation: 'I can see how this might be confusing – on the one hand there are some good things about your drinking and on the other hand you have some concerns'. This would be followed by asking clients if they thought there were any reasons for changing their drinking behaviour. After a note of the client's response is taken, the counsellor would ask the client to write these reasons into the relevant section of the notebook. 'The reasons I have to stop/cut down my drinking are:

1 ....
2 ....
3 ....
4 ....
5 ....
6 ....

Finally, clients can be asked to return a short time later (e.g. one or two hours or even on another day) after they have had the opportunity to review their record of the session and to add any other concerns they may have about their drinking. It is important to negotiate homework assignments to enable a continuation of the process outside of the counselling session. This would involve clients writing down assignments in their notebook to ensure recall and increase the probability of compliance. Homework would include reviewing (and outlining if appropriate) the concerns that clients have about their drinking and similarly reviewing 'reasons to change'. In addition, it would be useful to provide clients with a simple description of problem-solving which they could read in preparation for the next stage.

Problem-solving: putting intent into action

One of the factors that will reduce the possibility of relapse is the perception that 'I can do something about my problem'. Problem-solving techniques (see Chapter 4), described by D'Zurilla and Goldfried (1971) are particularly relevant in this regard. The counsellor could introduce clients to this technique by saying: 'We've discussed some of the reasons why you might want to cut down or stop drinking. What we're going to look at now is a technique that can be useful in helping you do so'.

While it is appropriate to conduct motivational interviewing on a one-to-one basis, the problem-solving process can be enhanced by having more than one client present. (A group approach to problem-solving is discussed in Chapter 7.) The following description assumes that *two* clients are involved in the programme. The counsellor would initially describe each step of problem-solving. In essence these are

1 problem identification
2 brainstorming of solutions
3 selection of best options
4 appraisal and evaluation of selected option(s)
5 deploying option(s).

Throughout, clients would be encouraged to view problems as challenges, rather than as insurmountable difficulties, and to adopt a 'have-a-go' attitude. This would be followed by the counsellor giving an example of the application of the technique on a problem generated by the counsellor. Each step would again be carefully explained. To generate interest, the counsellor could choose a humorous example and encourage each client to generate solutions.

These could be written on a whiteboard and then the counsellor would explain the decision-making process of selecting the best options.

Finally, the counsellor would negotiate selection of a 'low-risk' situation (identified from the assessment) for each client to practise the problem-solving technique upon. Both clients would take part in brainstorming and the response would be recorded on the whiteboard. However, only the client who had identified the problem would decide on the appropriate solution(s). The counsellor would then explain the value of rehearsing or practising a response before trying it out in real life, and that this would be the procedure in the current programme. Thus, each client will be introduced to problem-solving via written material, verbal description, modelling and practice. Clients should keep a record of the problem, the short-list of possible solutions and the final selected option(s) in their notebooks. Each client should go through this process at least once, emphasis being placed on teaching the technique as opposed to 'solving all the client's problems'.

The use of this intervention should be kept at a level commensurate with each client's learning abilities. In order to ensure success experiences it is appropriate to negotiate homework assignments whereby the client initially applies the problem-solving technique to 'low-risk' situations. This could include the agreement that the client would think through the solution, role-play it with a family member or friend, or put it into practice.

Where relevant, the counsellor could negotiate with each client to operationalize solutions selected as responses to problems generated in the counselling session. This would be conducted using goal-setting techniques. For example, if the suggested solution to the problem 'bored' was 'start fishing', the counsellor and client might agree on a goal such as 'go to the library and find a book on fishing' or 'renew my fishing licence'. Again the client would record this homework assignment in the notebook. When the client returns after a homework assignment it is pertinent to review and reinforce steps taken in the appropriate direction and identify factors that militate against success, such as unclear instructions on the homework assignment, or not understanding the problem-solving technique.

The problem-solving technique would then be focused upon the development of strategies to respond to challenges to the initial resolve to cut down or stop drinking. A number of tools can be used to develop individualized 'at risk' registers of 'high-risk' situations for each client, for example the Inventory of Drinking Situations (Annis 1986) and the Relapse Precipitants Inventory (Litman *et al*. 1985). These would be graded from least to most threatening. The counsellor would feed back information to each client about risky situations and ask, 'Is this accurate?' or 'Is there anything you would disagree with or like to see added?' To reinforce this exercise, both clients could then be asked to brainstorm specific examples of situations that would challenge their resolves to reduce or stop their alcohol use. The counsellor could record their responses on a whiteboard and clients might record personally relevant challenges in their notebook. The counsellor may then suggest that an appropriate way to respond to these situations will be by employing the problem-solving technique. To demonstrate this the counsellor would negotiate with each client the selection of a relatively low-risk situation and the problem-solving technique employed to generate solutions. The short-list of solutions would be recorded in the client's notebook and the selected solution cognitively (i.e. imagine going through the process) or behaviourally rehearsed.

The counsellor could note that, on this or any other session, if either client suggested solutions that the other thought pertinent to his or her own situation, then that client should feel free to record them and observe the other's resolution of the problem. Opportunity is thereby provided for learning by performance and by observation or modelling.

Next the counsellor would move away from immediately precipitating events and identify factors that might act as a warning of impending challenges to clients' resolves. The intention would be to encourage recognition that individual clients could anticipate challenges and that their own decision-making is of paramount importance. In line with Marlatt's description of Apparently Irrelevant Decisions (Marlatt and Gordon 1980) clients would be introduced to the idea that individuals may often deliberately choose to ignore warning signs or perhaps take deliberate action that would result in their entering a very high-risk situation.

Obviously such a suggestion might receive resistance from some clients. In order to overcome this resistance a description could be given of imaginary people and their actions leading to heavy drinking. In the script a large number of potential warnings would precede the people entering a high-risk situation and eventually drinking heavily. At a number of junctures they could have decided to move in a direction taking them away from risk.

Clients would be asked to listen to the script and identify any warning signs. When this has been done the counsellor should ask if alternatives, other than ending up drinking heavily, were available to the person. The counsellor would encourage clients to recognize the value of problem-solving in such situations.

Clients would then be asked if they believed that the imaginary people were responsible for their drinking behaviour and had indeed made a choice to drink. In our work we have found that clients tend to attribute a high degree of personal responsibility after this excercise. The counsellor could ask clients to identify similar situations that had occurred to them. 'What had occurred?' 'Had they been unable to cope or was there an element of choice?' Using such a procedure is likely to increase clients' acknowledgement that frequently they chose to ignore warning signs and that there is a strong element of personal responsibility in any resumption of heavy drinking. The counsellor should reinforce this acknowledgement of the role of personal decision-making.

Finally, clients could be asked to identify personally relevant 'warning signs'. These would be written on the whiteboard and subsequently recorded in the client's notebooks. The counsellor might ask: 'How can you respond to such warning signs in the future?' This is done to encourage clients to verbalize the value of problem-solving. The counsellor and each client might then select one personally relevant 'warning sign' and employ problem-solving methods to identify appropriate solutions. This would include behavioural or cognitive rehearsal.

From some use to heavy use

The next stage of a general relapse-prevention strategy would be devoted to responding to an initial 'slip' in resolve. Again it is likely that some clients would resist discussing this topic. Some would see this as an expression of a lack of faith or even condoning a return to heavy drinking.

In order to circumvent such resistance clients could be introduced to the analogy of a 'fire drill'. The counsellor would observe that a 'fire drill' does not condone, or increase, the risk of a fire occurring but does acknowledge that there is some risk. The preparation of a drill ensures that harm could be minimized if such an event occurred. Thus it is also wise to have a 'relapse drill', since relapse is a possibility.

Clients would be asked to identify what factors (internal and external) may encourage them to continue drinking or drug-using after an initial 'slip' in their resolve. The procedure used earlier would be appropriate: clients would call out relevant factors and these would be recorded by the counsellor on to a whiteboard. Clients would then record personally relevant responses in their notebooks.

The counsellor could help identify specific rather than general factors by asking clients to give examples of actual occurrences. If a client said 'feeling guilty' the counsellor could ask the client to give a detailed example of this occurring. The counsellor would ask, 'How could you respond to these?', thereby encouraging clients to recognize the relevance of the problem-solving technique. The identified factors would be presented as problems to be solved. This method facilitates clients' recognizing that factors associated with continued use are specific and reversible rather than global and irreversible. Thus 'slips' are within the individual's range of control. To reinforce this perception, the counsellor and each client could negotiate the selection of one of the personally relevant factors and employ the problem-solving technique to generate possible solutions.

The counsellor would conclude by noting that while 'stopping once started' may be difficult, there are strategies that can be employed to reduce risk and harm, and it is possible to get back on track. The counsellor would then explain that the next part of the programme would be devoted to developing a 'relapse drill'.

Clients would be asked to 'brainstorm' strategies that could help them stop or cut down their drinking use after an initial 'slip'. The counsellor should direct responses to be specific and detailed. For example, 'Call someone' could be deemed an inappropriate response. The counsellor might encourage the client, saying 'Good idea. Who might you call?' 'What's their telephone number?' 'What will they do?' 'How will they help?'

This could be followed by the negotiation of a contract wherein the client agrees to contact the specified friend and plan how this person might help. Potential action would then be rehearsed with, for example, the counsellor role-playing the friend. Each client then similarly rehearses a number of responses. As usual clients should keep a record in their notebooks and consequently have available a personally relevant 'relapse drill'. Thus clients have the opportunity to identify, plan and rehearse specific responses.

Finally, brief discussion might be given to the role of decision-making, the counsellor reminding clients of their earlier discussion of the issue. The counsellor would ask the clients to describe why people continued drinking heavily, encouraging them to verbalize the importance of decision-making as well as any skill deficits.

In order to provide the opportunity for clients to increase their self-efficacy and rehearse their skills, the counsellor might now negotiate the selection of a subjectively challenging, but not overwhelming, high-risk situation. This would be identified on the basis of information from the initial assessment, the counsellor's perception of the client's performance and negotiation with the individual client.

Such situations will obviously vary for different clients: for example, walking past an alcohol retailers, going into an off-licence to purchase non-alcoholic goods, or spending time socializing in a public house. Before undertaking their agreed tasks clients should be encouraged to identify the risks associated with each situation and to employ the problem-solving technique as an aid to planning strategies to ensure a non-drinking or non-heavy drinking outcome. This would be facilitated by clients cognitively and behaviourally rehearsing strategies before leaving the therapeutic setting. Personal responsibility, decision-making and use of skills should be emphasized as crucial determinants of outcome. Clients would then be encouraged to give it a try. It is important to stress that all the situations should be carefully chosen to be testing but not over-whelming and to result in a 'success-experience' being achieved.

On completion of the exercise clients would then return for a brief review of their performance. This would include identification of any difficulties and verbal reinforcement for the application of appropriate strategies. Throughout this session the counsellor should emphasize internal attribution of outcome.

In addition, it is important that clients be encouraged to avoid over-generalization of success leading to an unrealistic perception of personal competence. It might be suggested that deliberately and continually putting oneself at risk is unwise, but that it would be useful to anticipate and plan responses to risks encountered in everyday living. Thus clients would employ strategies learned through the programme culminating in a success experience in a real-life challenge designed to increase their self-efficacy. The importance of identifying specific risks and planning will also have been emphasized.

Review and reappraisal

The final part of any relapse-prevention strategy should include a review of the preceding interventions, including a reconsideration of why the clients wanted to change. This review would involve asking the clients to reiterate their reasons (and add any additional ones) for changing their drinking behaviour. It could also include encouraging the clients to describe the problem-solving technique and outline what factors may challenge their initial resolve to quit. Clients might note how they would meet these challenges (e.g. by using the problem-solving method and careful decision-making) and they could also describe their 'relapse drill'. If there were any areas where the clients appear unsure, the counsellor could help them find the appropriate part in their notebook and briefly take them through the relevant details or even set up revision sessions. Clients could be urged to help each other through this process.

Finally, clients could be introduced to a decision matrix as described by Marlatt (Marlatt and Gordon 1980). This would be used to help the clients review and enhance the initial decision to change. The matrix consists of the pros and cons, short and long term, of returning to heavy drinking versus staying stopped or keeping alcohol consumption low. The counsellor would review these with each client, acknowledging both the costs and benefits of change and encouraging the clients to recognize these factors as influences on their decision to drink heavily or not. This links into the initial motivational interviewing session where the clients expressed their rationale for changing their drinking behaviour. To conclude, the counsellor would negotiate with the clients that they would employ the decision matrix in the future if they became aware of challenges to, or changes in, their resolve to abstain or cut down.

The counsellor would usually end by suggesting that after leaving, the clients should refer to their notebooks to help them remember the contents of the sessions and to help them deploy strategies to keep their resolutions to change.

Intervention strategies aimed at attenuating the risk of relapse, similar to those outlined above, have been subjected to experimental investigation (Allsop *et al.* forthcoming). In brief, clients going through the programme took significantly longer to relapse and overall did better than either a no-additional-treatment control or a relapse-discussion-based group. It should be noted, however, that while these individually tailored procedures did help, the gains were eroded over time and the very significant differences reported at six-months follow-up were less evident at one year. The implications of this are probably twofold. First, booster-sessions may be of value, especially if provided at the three to six month mark. Second, and perhaps more importantly, we need to address the nature of our clients' environments. All the resolution-enhancement, problem-solving techniques, self-efficacy boosting and skill-development exercises cannot be expected to overcome hostile relationships and inimical social circumstances ranging from long-term unemployment to abject poverty. As Perry and Jessor (1986) have noted, clinicians often work as though their techniques can inoculate clients against long-term deprivation, whereas in fact such thinking is little better than blaming the victim for not being skilled enough to cope with the intolerable. Relapse prevention work needs to be undertaken with a very real appreciation of the environment in which clients live their lives. However, a 'success story' is included to demonstrate that in spite of social difficulties people can make the break.

Case study   Overcoming relapse

Don is an unemployed 36-year-old man who had not worked for eight years. When presenting for treatment, he was consuming approximately 130 units in a typical drinking week and was a regular user of valium. He occasionally experienced 'en bloc' blackouts, reported 'relief drinking' most days, was relatively highly dependent on alcohol, had many arrests for alcohol-related offences, suffered from pancreatitis and duodenal ulcers and had been referred for treatment to the Alcohol Treatment Unit (ATU) on four occasions over the previous six years.

After all his previous admissions, Don had left the hospital and commenced drinking again within a few days. The ATU staff considered him a 'difficult case', who was reluctant to 'give his drinking up'. In terms of Prochaska and DiClemente's model he might be considered to be somewhere between 'pre-contemplation' and 'contemplation'. After completing the programme, contact was maintained with Don over a twelve-month period. After six months, he was interviewed to assess his progress. At that time he reported that he had had no alcohol at all since he had left the unit. This was accompanied by reported improvements in other areas of his life. He was 'more settled', 'more relaxed', 'less depressed', 'sleeping better', and 'feeling healthier'. He also reported a radical change in his use of tranquillizers both during the day and at night, to the extent that he was using them only in specific situations and had used them only twice in the month prior to the follow-up interview. His general appearance was much improved as compared to the initial interview. When questioned about this change he reported: 'The help that M. [the nurse] gave me was good. Probably most of why I'm okay was because of that problem-solving stuff. And before no one had let me look at my problems without pushing me – I was part of what happened – I opened up and wouldn't stop. I've got reasons to stay off the bevvy.'

Don claimed that he had never before been asked to think about what worried him about his drinking. When encouraged by the nurse he had recognized a litany of reasons for change. Practising the problem-solving method then helped him feel 'more in control now. More confident. I can handle things better now.' For example, he reported that he had moved from his father's house (his father was a very heavy drinker) to live with his brother (a very modest drinker) and there was an agreement that he would leave if he started to drink again. Don attributed his decision to move to the problem-solving techniques. He said that on previous occasions of trying to stop drinking he had returned home and immediately felt the pressures to drink. He therefore sat down and 'thought up ways of sorting this. I decided to move. All the other things I thought of were difficult. Moving helped.' Using the same techniques, he built up new interests. For example, he acquired a huge hound which took up a great deal of his time. It also provided him with some contingent reinforcement in that he reasoned that he would lose the dog if he started to drink again. He also reported using the technique in potentially risky situations. One example illustrates this. He had begun to feel fed up and started to 'feel like a drink. I couldn't get it out of my head.' He decided that he would go for a 'few drinks'. However, half-way to the public house, he stopped himself and thought of the situation as a problem. He concluded that drinking was 'a useless solution' and decided to take a walk instead with his gigantic dog – 'I walked for miles. I walked the urge off.' This increased his confidence that he could 'do something about urges'.

It was apparent throughout the interview that Don still felt very conscious of risk and was by no means complacent. Indeed, he was 'fed up with everyone telling me I'm doing okay. It's still hard work'. In order to assess his reported use of the problem-solving technique, Don was asked to describe its use, and the steps involved, in one of the situations he had described. He reported 'thinking up lots of solutions', 'choosing one', 'thinking if it was any good' and 'doing it', a very reasonable description of the technique utilized in the strategy.

Conclusion

To paraphrase Prochaska and DiClemente (1986), what we hope that this outlining of relapse-prevention and management strategies has achieved, is to allow such endeavour at least to approach the cognitive and behavioural complexity of our clients. For too long the area of relapse has been predicated on simplistic and unhelpful self-fulfilling prophecies, of which 'One drink –one drunk' is a prime example. An appreciation of the Prochaska and DiClemente model ensures that slogans are replaced by more sophisticated methods that address the difficulties and complexities under consideration.

In conclusion it is worth while to step briefly away from the restricted enclave of relapse and addiction and consider a broader issue. In psychological and medical research there is a choice to be made between studying abnormality or illness as opposed to normality or well-being. While the first options initially appear attractive, it has to be remembered (or in fact learned) that health is not merely the absence of illness or normality the mirror image of abnormality. The epidemiology of well-being informs us that many factors – individual, financial, social, economic and political – dictate and influence health. Studying ill people can inform us only on how the disease under study progresses and perhaps how it may be treated. In order both to prevent and to treat a condition a comprehensive understanding of why people do not succumb is also vital. After all it is much easier to fix a malfunctioning engine or defective piece of equipment if one has a knowledge of how they function when working properly. Without a workshop manual, the task is often little better than a lottery of guesses. Similarly one's understanding of relapse needs to be informed by knowledge of successful behaviour change.

Paradoxically from the perspective of relapse the very value of Prochaska and DiClemente's model is that relapse is not included as either a stage or a process. What examination of the stages of change model tells us is how the succeeders do it, which is of course vital information for all attempting to change, because it highlights all the areas where things can go wrong. Thus in future studies investigators concerned with relapse need a well-developed interest in those that give up their problematic behaviours, rather than in those that give in to the temptation of their old ways. The Prochaska and DiClemente model, and we hope the discussions in this chapter, give testimony and support to Litman's (1980) apposite comment that 'complex behaviours like relapse do not lend themselves readily to simple models'.

References

Allsop, S. and Saunders, B. (1988) 'The effectiveness of relapse programmes', in F. Brin and N. Solowij (eds) *Proceedings of the National Drug and Alcohol Research Centre: Annual Symposium*, Sydney: University of New South Wales, December.

Allsop, S., Saunders, B. and Carr, A. (forthcoming) 'Relapse prevention: a controlled trial with problem drinkers'.

Annis, H. (1986) 'A relapse prevention model for treatment of alcoholics', in W.R. Miller and N. Heather (eds) *Treating Addictive Behaviours: Process of Change*, New York: Plenum Press.

Azrin, N. (1976) 'Improvements in the community: reinforcement approach to alcoholism', *Behaviour Research and Therapy* 14: 339–48.

Chaney, E., O'Leary, M. and Marlatt, G. (1978) 'Skill training with alcoholics', *Journal of Consulting and Clinical Psychology* 46: 1,092–104.

Condiotte, M. and Lichenstein, E. (1981) 'Self efficacy and relapse in smoking cessation programs', *Journal of Consulting and Clinical Psychology* 49: 648–58.

D'Zurilla, T. and Goldfried, M. (1971) 'Problem solving and behaviour modification', *Journal of Abnormal Psychology* 78: 107–26.

Edwards, G. (1987) 'Book review of *Relapse Prevention* by G. Marlatt and J. Gordon (eds)', *British Journal of Addiction* 82: 319–23.

Lichenstein, E. and Weiss, S. (1986) 'Task Force 3: patterns of smoking relapse', *Health Psychology* 5 (suppl.): 29–40.

Litman, G. (1980) 'Relapse in alcoholism: traditional and current approaches', in G. Edwards and M. Grant (eds) *Alcoholism Treatment in Transition*, London: Croom Helm.

Litman, G., Stapleton, J., Oppenheimer, A., Peleg, M. and Jackson, P. (1985) 'Situations related to alcoholism relapse', *British Journal of Addiction* 78: 581–9.

Marlatt, G. and Gordon, J. (1980) 'Determinants of relapse: implications for the maintenance of behaviour change', in P. Davidson and S. Davidson (eds) *Medicine Changing Health Lifestyles*, New York: Brunner/Mazel.

Miller, W.R. (1983) 'Motivational interviewing with problem drinkers', *Behavioural Psychotherapy* 11: 147–72.

Perry, C. and Jessor, R. (1986) 'The concept of health promotion and the prevention of adolescent drug abuse', *Health Education Quarterly* 12, 2: 169–84.

Prochaska, J.O. and DiClemente, C.C. (1986) 'Towards a comprehensive model of change', in W.R. Miller and N. Heather (eds) *Treating Addictive Behaviours: Process of Change*, New York: Plenum Press.

Rankin, H. (1986) 'Dependence and compulsion: experimental models of change', in W.R. Miller and N. Heather (eds) *Treating Addictive Behaviours: Process of Change*, New York: Plenum Press.

Saunders, B. and Allsop, S. (1987) 'Relapse: a psychological perspective', *British Journal of Addiction* 82: 417–29.

Shiffman, S. (1986) 'Task Force 2: models of smoking relapse', *Health Psychology* 5 (suppl.): 13–27.

Stewart, T. (1987) *The Heroin Users*, London: Routledge & Kegan Paul.

Sutton, S. (1987) 'Social-psychological approaches to understanding addictive behaviours: attitude-behaviour and decision-making models', *British Journal of Addiction* 82, 4: 355–70.

Part two

Issues in service delivery

Chapter six

Alcohol counselling in context

Stephen Rollnick and Ian MacEwan

One of the refreshing features of the stages of change model is its breadth of application. It provides a framework for using a wide range of strategies with many different kinds of drinkers. These drinkers occur in all kinds of settings. The pre-contemplator who approaches a general practitioner with stomach problems, the young mother who hesitantly talks to a social worker about her use of alcohol in the face of isolation and poor housing, the man who telephones an alcohol counselling service because his wife insists that he does something about his drinking, the relapser who returns to the front door of the hostel for problem drinkers – these are some of the commonly occurring manifestations of problem drinking in the community.

The settings in which these problems arise are more than just buildings which serve a particular purpose; they provide a context in which alcohol problems are usually dealt with in a particular way. What happens when the stages of change model is used in these settings? How much do the settings themselves have to change? What problems arise and how can they be overcome?

The aim of this chapter is to explore the use of the stages of change model in three different settings. In each case we shall briefly describe the setting, identify a key issue posed by the application of the model, and then turn to a number of practical questions which need to be considered in that setting.

Community-based counselling services

The setting

Community-based counselling services have a common origin in the disease model which emerged in the 1960s to deal with the disabling effects of chronic problem drinking. Often linked to hospital-based treatment units and associated AA groups, they developed a structure and orientation which still survive in some agencies today: a small number of committed counsellers in an under-funded agency providing one-to-one counselling to drinkers struggling to maintain abstinence.

In recent years, particularly in the UK, these services have diversified because the disease model has been replaced by a broader model which views problem drinking on a continuum, affecting many more people than those usually labelled 'alcoholics'. Therefore, counselling services cannot possibly deal with the scale of the problem by merely offering one-to-one counselling appointments. Training and support is needed for primary care workers like doctors, social workers and health visitors to deal with problem drinking in the course of their everyday work.

Today, considerable variety exists in the orientation of community-based services; some remain embedded in the one-to-one model described above, while others have focused on the training of primary care workers. It is important to note that the stages of change model falls directly in line with the broader view of problem drinking which has emerged over the last fifteen or twenty years (Heather and Robertson 1985). A wide range of people get into difficulty with alcohol; their problems vary in severity and they do not necessarily present themselves to counselling services as ready to do something about a clearly defined problem. The stages of change model allows us to categorize these people in terms of their understanding of their drink-related problems, and it provides clear guidelines for counselling them, but how can the structure and orientation of community-based counselling services be designed accordingly?

Moving beyond the action-stage orientation

Many community-based services have been severely constrained by what we might call the 'action-stage orientation', a therapeutic model which is geared primarily towards those at the action stage. Potential clients for these services exist at all stages of change; this should be evident from a reading of the first part of this book. Yet many of the facilities which developed in the 1960s and 1970s followed the model developed in specialized in-patient units and focused their energies on patients who were assumed to be at the action stage. Drinkers were offered time-limited treatment and then discharged into what is sometimes still called 'after-care', a period in which apparently less help is needed because the drinker has successfully negotiated a transition to abstinence.

This orientation runs into understandable difficulties among drinkers on either side of the action stage itself. Those at the contemplation stage, for example (see Miller and Rollnick in preparation), for whom ambivalence about change is a central problem, might well be reluctant to accept the need for lifelong abstinence, and might not come forward with solutions to the problem, since these are both action stage issues. These drinkers could then be labelled as unmotivated clients, and develop relationship problems with counsellors who view this resistance as a sign of reluctance to accept the seriousness of the problem (Miller 1983; Rollnick 1985). So too, clients at the maintenance stage who succeed with initial behaviour change might be left feeling unsupported because they are viewed as successes and possibly even 'discharged'.

It is a clear implication of the model developed in this book that services need to move beyond the action-stage orientation and embrace drinkers at all stages of change; some of them have moved a long way in this direction. For example, a Community Alcohol Team described by Clement (1987) focused only upon training primary care workers to pick up pre-contemplators and contemplators in their everyday work. No face-to-face counselling was offered. Some services, however, still remain completely embedded in the action-stage orientation described above. The majority lie somewhere between these two poles.

Moving beyond the action-stage orientation implies change on a number of fronts. Specialist counsellors and primary care workers need to be trained to deal with drinkers at different stages, and the role of volunteers needs to be reconsidered; these will be dealt with in turn in this chapter.

Practical questions

How should counsellors be trained?

The first part of this book describes numerous strategies that can be used with different clients. It is based upon the principle that counselling problem drinkers involves using a wide range of clinical skills and that these skills should be studied by counsellors and practised on an ongoing basis. Where does this leave the staff of a busy community-based service and the primary care workers they wish to train?

Turning first to specialist alcohol counsellors, it is a characteristic of community-based agencies that the pressure of work often forces them to neglect their own training needs. If counsellors do not spend time thinking about their work and trying out new ideas, their work will become stagnant. Time needs to be set aside for this activity, even if this means a cut-back in the overall output of the team. Going away on specialist courses can certainly be a useful introduction to concepts and strategies, but it lacks the continuity necessary for linking these new ideas to everyday clinical work. Training alcohol counsellors is an ongoing process. If drinkers are not 'cured' just because they have succeeded with initial behaviour change, then alcohol counsellors are not 'trained' just because they have completed a course, seen 100 clients or gained promotion.

One of the most productive training formats for specialist counsellors is the review of ongoing cases. The model described in this book can be used as a framework for guiding discussion in a small group format, ideally with an outside facilitator. Among the questions which could be raised about a client are: At what stage of change is this person? How does he or she view the problem? Is this different from the counsellor's view? Is this person ambivalent about a change in drinking habits (see Chapter 2)? If so, what is the nature of this ambivalence? What can the counsellor do to help this person come to terms with the dilemma? (See Miller and Rollnick in preparation.) At what pace should the counsellor be working with this client? What strategies, in the broadest sense of the word, could the counsellor use? Should the counsellor be spending time with the client in the community, helping with specific problems like coping with walking past pubs, and so on?

It would be claiming too much for the stages of change model to suggest that all clinical problems can be discussed within this format. Sometimes, for example, irrespective of the stage of change, a drinker will be feeling depressed, and the counsellor will need to understand and work with this sadness in a constructive way. Nevertheless, this framework is probably one of the most useful for structuring the majority of case discussions, however these are organized within the team.

Turning now to the training of primary care workers, a different set of challenges emerge: how can specialist staff communicate the stages of change framework to people who have less time, and usually considerably less interest in the whole subject of problem drinking. Here we find grounds for both optimism and despair! On the one hand, independent of the stages of change model, the whole subject of training primary care workers is a complex and difficult business. It is beyond the scope of this discussion even to outline the major issues involved; a useful review can be found in Clement (1987). One conclusion that does emerge, however, is that it is probably best to initiate training among those who have the time available, who have the support of their managers, who want and need the skills and who are able to use the skills acquired in their everyday work. Otherwise the training initiative is likely to end in failure. Another general guidance is that, as with our clients, it is best to teach people skills as close as possible to the environment in which they will be needed. Exactly what kind of training is done will therefore depend on the context. Social workers on a child care team, for example, might benefit from a regular review of cases under the supervision of a specialist counsellor; general practitioners, on the other hand, might benefit more from access to written guidelines, and self-help material which they can use with their patients.

On the optimistic side, the stages of change framework can be of considerable value in developing training programmes for primary care workers. It provides a clear rationale for this work: to help them identify drinkers at different stages of change. This means that they will need to be sensitive to the problem of ambivalence which so often characterizes the drinker in trouble, particularly at the contemplation stage; they will also need to be aware of some of the strategies that can be used with drinkers at the action and maintenance stages, and they will need to consider carefully the question of whether to intervene themselves, consult the specialists, or initiate a direct referral.

How should volunteers be deployed?

A number of converging trends in the alcohol field (see Orford 1987) have led to the deployment of volunteer counsellors and the setting up of training schemes. One of the obvious applications of the stages of change model is in the training of these counsellors. They too, like the specialist counsellors, need to be responsive to the needs of different drinkers at different stages. Much of the contents of the first part of this book could be integrated into their training courses. More complex, however, is the policy decision about how to deploy volunteers in the first place. Why have they usually been trained only to work as one-to-one counsellors, as extra hands for coping with the case-load in the agency counselling rooms? Since maintenance and social support are such key issues for problem drinkers, why are volunteers not encouraged to work in the community, visiting and supporting drinkers on a more active basis? Why are they not deployed to 'help with' pre-contemplators who don't come forward to the agency itself, but who appear in the everyday work-load of primary care workers?

There are at least two main reasons for the exclusive deployment of volunteers as one-to-one counsellors. First, it is probably assumed that they enjoy counselling more than visiting drinkers in their homes or working under supervision in the primary care setting. Second, agencies themselves, under pressure to get help with the immediate case-load, simply slot the volunteers into this gap, sometimes because they are still struggling with a demand-led service which has its origin in the action-stage orientation of the traditional specialist service.

Developing a wider role for volunteers will require careful consideration of the options available. It is quite likely that recruitment itself will need to have a different orientation. Some volunteers might like to help with transport, some might wish to help drinkers actively learn to cope with difficult situations like going into a pub, some might wish to help run training programmes, some might enjoy constructing self-help material, while others might want to work as one-to-one counsellors.

General practice and general hospitals

Hospital and general practice settings are clearly different from the community services discussed above. The excessive drinkers do not necessarily identify themselves as clients needing specialist help, and the staff involved, mostly doctors and nurses, are not alcohol specialists. Many of the problems discussed in this section stem from this basic observation. The counselling approach described in this book cannot be used in these settings without carefully considering the clinical environment in which the drinkers appear.

The settings

It would be wrong to describe these settings as full of 'alcoholics' or people with serious drinking problems. However, they do have many heavy or excessive drinkers passing through their doors, some of whom have more serious alcohol-related problems. Although the published statistics vary, not least because researchers use different definitions of excessive or problem drinking and are applying the definitions to different populations, the number involved would appear to vary between 10 and 30 per cent for men, and less among women.

From the doctors' and nurses' point of view, lack of time can be a problem. Those in the primary health care setting see patients for ten to fifteen minutes at a time, although contact can be maintained over a period of months or years, while those in the hospital setting have the drinker in bed for days or weeks at a time, yet face continuity problems once the person is discharged. In both settings, the personnel are busy and have other priorities, alcohol seldom being near the top of the list.

From the drinkers' point of view, alcohol is not always on the top of their agenda either. It might be a medical or social problem that brings them into contact with health personnel, which may or may not be related to drinking. Seldom do they present with a request for help with a drink-specific problem. They will therefore not be uniformly receptive to counselling or advice, although the existence of some form of medical crisis clearly provides a good opportunity for intervention. Studies in both settings appear to confirm the value of what has come to be known as brief or minimal intervention (Chick *et al.* 1985; Wallace *et al.* 1988; Heather 1989).

In summary, drinkers in these settings are clearly a heterogeneous group. They will appear at all stages of change. The challenge for those developing alcohol intervention packages is to marry the practical reality faced by clients and staff with the sensitive use of a counselling model which accommodates drinkers with different needs, at different stages of change. There are good reasons to feel optimistic about this endeavour, since the brief intervention projects noted above appear to have motivated drinkers to change *without* matching the intervention to the person's stage of change.

Redefining the nature of problem drinking

For those working in hospital and general practice settings it has become necessary, and indeed worth while, to employ a new model of problem drinking. It is a truism about any treatment that the model used by the practitioner will vitally affect the relationship with the patients and their reactions to the encounter. This issue has been highlighted in many discussions of the problems associated with traditional alcohol counselling (see Miller 1983; Rollnick 1985). The medical model of alcoholism has, until fairly recently, been the most widely accepted framework available to doctors and nurses. Given the kind of setting described above, it is not difficult to see how the use of this model will lead health personnel into a minefield of clinical problems. Quite simply, the model does not fit the clinical reality. Most people who run into difficulty with alcohol do not approach the stereotype of an alcoholic. They lie somewhere in the murky area between moderate drinking and severe dependence on alcohol. It is therefore not surprising, as Thom and Tellez (1986) found in their interview study, that GPs find it difficult to draw the line between problem and non-problem drinking. Finally, because the term 'alcoholic' is so often associated with failure and social disgrace, it is not surprising that drinkers appear unwilling to enter into a discussion about this topic with a doctor.

This rather bleak analysis contrasts sharply with the optimism surrounding the use of a new model of problem drinking which has emerged in general hospital and general practice settings (see Anderson 1987; Chick *et al.* 1985; Wallace *et al.* 1988; Rollnick 1987). In essence, excessive drinking is viewed on a continuum from moderate to severe, and the stages of change framework is used to categorize people and identify priorities for counselling (see Anderson 1987). Using this framework, it is argued, doctors and nurses should be able to identify excessive drinkers and counsel them in the course of their everyday work, without getting bogged down in the kind of conceptual and clinical problems associated with the disease model. Alcohol is viewed as a general health issue affecting large numbers of ordinary people. No reference need be made to the term 'alcoholic', and moderate drinking is more commonly used as a drinking goal than lifelong abstinence. Counselling is brief and non-specialist and, using the stages of change model, no assumption is made that drinkers should be at the action stage, ready to do something about their drinking. If they are at an earlier stage the counselling takes a different form, usually centring on the less-directive process of helping the individual explore the links between consumption and problems, and identifying the pros and cons of change (see Chapter 3).

Even with this new model of problem drinking, it would be unwise to assume that the use of a stages of change model in these settings will be problem free. Rather, a new set of problems emerges. The discussion below serves to identify some of these. Essentially they revolve around the question of how to provide counselling in a sensitive and appropriate manner.

Practical questions

How should pre-contemplators be approached?

Some pre-contemplators have very serious alcohol problems, like the man admitted to a medical ward with liver cirrhosis who has never thought about doing something about the problem. There is no doubt here about the validity of a counselling exercise. Such cases, however, are a minority among pre-contemplators. The majority are not seriously dependent on alcohol and have few or no problems directly associated with their drinking. They are at-risk heavy drinkers.

How to deal with these pre-contemplators is important because they probably represent a significant percentage of the excessive drinkers found in these settings. For example, if one defines pre-contemplators as people who do not acknowledge that they drink too much, as we did in an unpublished Cardiff postal survey of male general practice patients, well over half (66 per cent) of the 146 excessive drinkers fell into this category. The same questionnaire and question used in a general hospital survey produced a figure of 30 per cent among 170 excessive drinkers.

If pre-contemplators do not think that they are drinking too much, let alone feel the need to do something about it, should such people be brought into counselling? Is counselling the right word for such an encounter which does not involve individuals identifying themselves as having a problem? What effect will a discussion about drinking have on the counsellor and this kind of client? Are such clients less responsive to counselling? Unfortunately the answers to these questions have yet to emerge from a field which is still in its infancy. Nevertheless, it seems highly likely that the administration of advice to all pre-contemplators will result in miscommunication, a problem identified in Heather's (1987) description of the DRAMS project in Scotland.

For example, consider the case of a male excessive drinker who is confronted by a doctor because of a high consumption level. When asked about this he replies: 'No, doctor, I can't see any problem. I drink the same as all my mates.' The risk of communication breakdown is now fairly high; the doctor might well reach the conclusion that the drinker is denying the problem and lacking in motivation; in turn, the drinker might feel an invasion of personal liberty and become defensive and unresponsive to advice. These are precisely the difficulties sometimes experienced in the treatment of more serious alcohol problems, which Miller (1983) has attributed to the use of an inappropriate model of counselling. The client is viewed as having negative characteristics – like denial and poor motivation – when in fact there is a poor fit between the model of counselling being used and the reality of the client (see Rollnick 1985). In this example, the doctor is confronted by what is in effect a social norm ('We all drink four or five pints a session') while using a model based on the personal pathology of the drinker ('You have a problem').

If these kinds of pre-contemplators are living in an economically deprived area, the chances are that they will have approached the doctor with some combination of medical, social and psychological problems. Excessive drinking is by no means the most important problem. In fact the drinker might well feel that alcohol is the one form of recreation which provides some release from the pressures of everyday life. Some doctors would understandably regard it as clinically insensitive to suggest to such people that they now have another problem which they should do something about.

Until detailed research is conducted on the process of counselling, it would be premature to conclude that this kind of pre-contemplator should be left out of intervention altogether. However, it might also be premature to suggest that busy health workers will be doing 'good work' by screening and 'advising' all pre-contemplators they come across. If giving advice means telling people that they drink too much and that they should cut down, then health workers might experience failure and disillusionment. As seen in the above example, prospective clients might well become hostile and unco-operative. By definition, drinkers at the pre-contemplation stage are not ready for action; telling them what to do runs against the basic principles of the model described in this book.

Instead of 'giving advice' to pre-contemplators, or making them feel that they should do something about their drinking, health workers should adopt a much more modest goal, one which is perfectly compatible with the stages of change model: encourage people to start thinking about their behaviour (see Anderson 1987). If the pre-contemplator has a drink-related problem this might well provide a meaningful context for discussion (Rollnick 1987). The difficulty, however, is that getting people to think about their behaviour, without making them feel that you want them to do something about it, is a delicate matter; it is not 'counselling', because the person has not come forward with a problem; it is not 'advice-giving', because the person is clearly not ready for it; it is perhaps best described as 'sowing the seed', a term often used by doctors to describe a delicate interaction of this kind.

How can prescriptive advice-giving be avoided?

Doctors and nurses are used to telling people what to do. It is part of their everyday work with concrete medical problems. A prescriptive approach has unfortunately been reinforced by the tendency in the literature to link smoking counselling with alcohol counselling (see Wallace *et al.* 1988). Reference is often made to the large-scale smoking study by Russell *et al.* (1979) in which it is argued that if all GPs gave advice to all smokers, then many thousands would stop smoking across the country, even if the majority of those counselled by any one doctor remain un-responsive. The national gain is more important than the individual losses, even if these are in the majority. The same rationale has been used to encourage GPs to engage all excessive drinkers in advice-giving (Wallace *et al.* 1988). Although politically attractive, this could encourage the kind of prescriptive advice-giving which will lead to serious communication breakdown with drinkers. Excessive drinkers are not necessarily the same as smokers; the most import-ant difference between these groups is that drinkers are less likely to view their behaviour as problematic.

Fortunately the foundations for a generally less prescriptive approach to drinkers have already been laid. The stages of change framework forms an important part of the model presented to GPs by the Royal College of General Practitioners and described in Anderson's (1987) review of general practice alcohol counselling. The challenge facing alcohol specialists is to communicate this model to doctors and nurses. The acquisition of a range of negotiating and counselling skills will be the best way to avoid the problem of prescriptive advice-giving.

Should intervention be alcohol specific?

Counsellors who work with severely dependent drinkers have daily contact with problems caused by the perceived stigma associated with having a drinking problem. Less dependent excessive drinkers in a hospital or health centre setting will be just as sensitive, if not more so, to the possibility of being stigmatized.

Non-attendance and drop-out among excessive drinkers in brief intervention programmes are fairly widely reported in the liter-ature. Before attributing this to 'unresponsive patients' or 'natural wastage', it is possible that the alcohol-specific nature of the intervention is a problem for people who are concerned about being stigmatized, particularly the pre-contemplators. Among the alter-natives available are a fitness test or a health check. In the mailed survey (noted above) male drinkers in a general practice setting in Cardiff, were asked about getting help for all sorts of health and personal problems. While only 24 per cent of the 146 excessive drinkers said they wanted help to reduce drinking – many of them being severely dependent drinkers who had received help in the past – 62 per cent said they would like help to improve fitness. When asked about different kinds of help for fitness, a fitness test in the health centre was by far the most popular choice. Related to the fitness test is the general idea of a health check, something which has been explored in the general practice setting by Stott and Pill (1988), who studied the problem of non-attendance in some detail. In the drinking field the health check has been used in the outcome study conducted by Kristenson and his colleagues (Kristenson *et al.* 1983).

Whether one is thinking about a fitness test, a health check, or a doctor or nurse approaching the subject of drinking in the course of everyday consultations in a less stigmatizing manner, there is clearly much to be gained from a more careful study of different forms of minimal intervention in hospital and general practice settings.

Hostels for problem drinkers

The setting

The number of hostels for problem drinkers has increased steadily over the last twenty years. What unites them is the need to provide residential stability for people with drinking problems who might otherwise have difficulty controlling their drinking in the face of homelessness or the threat of it.

Despite some variation in organization and orientation, their similarities are more notable than their differences. They are usually staffed by people with a social work or nursing background, and sometimes by people who themselves have struggled with a drinking problem. These workers usually have no prior training in alcohol studies. The clients enter the hostel environment for a range of reasons, not just because they want to resolve a drinking problem: poverty, loneliness, hunger, fear, homelessness or the threat of it, attention from the police, bailiffs, or plain despair at being trapped in some circle without apparent exit are all common and legitimate reasons for referral. In summary, the reason for seeking this kind of residential care is as often asylum as it is reform.

The orientation of hostels is usually firmly abstinence-based: people are mostly required to be abstinent before admission, as an indication of their motivation to change. The kind of client sought is therefore an 'alcoholic', and ideally someone who does not have the complications of a mental illness, who has no record of violence, and who has a desire to live communally for a period of weeks or months while they attempt to resolve their drinking problem.

The programme content of most hostels is based on the medical model and Alcoholics Anonymous, with an emphasis on group meetings which affirm the need to come to terms with the seriousness of the drinking problem and the need for lifelong abstinence. Some hostels have also developed a stronger psychotherapeutic orientation, not unlike that maintained in therapeutic communities. In general, there is a tendency for hostels to use a single programme, albeit with different components, which all residents are encouraged to make use of.

Developing an individual approach in a communal setting

The stages of change framework has much potential in hostel settings, since staff usually have the opportunity to work with individual clients over a period of weeks or even months. Ironically, of all the settings reviewed in this chapter, hostels might need to change the most in order to accommodate this framework.

Underlying this paradox is the reality of the hostel environment, an institutional atmosphere in which the very antithesis of an individualized approach is often practised. Residents are obliged to conform to a fairly strict set of house rules relating to standards of behaviour, drinking practices and attendance at group meetings. The hostel itself is often isolated from the very world in which the drinking problems arose – and in which these problems eventually will have to be solved. In brief, the residents are at risk of becoming institutionalized.

In addition to these environmental factors, the therapeutic programme in many hostels centres around the 'action-stage orientation'; as discussed in the section on community-based services, this orientation seriously undermines the flexibility of the programme to adapt to the needs of the individual. Hostel programmes of this kind can often become rigid and inflexible, with staff paying little attention to research findings or other approaches used in the field.

It is unlikely that one particular style of programme will be suitable for every client seeking residential treatment. It is not the purpose of this exercise to address the issue of matching client to intervention strategy but rather to promote the need for programmes to be flexible, to offer a range of interventions and to work with clients at their current positions in the stages of change framework. Programmes need to adjust to clients and not the other way around.

The stages of change framework provides a structure in which workers can use a wide range of approaches, including strategies like harm-reduction for pre-contemplators and contemplators, relapse-prevention for maintainers, and relapse management and damage limitation for relapsers. To accommodate this kind of flexibility might require substantial changes in the orientation of a hostel.

Practical questions

How can change be introduced into a hostel?

Given the complexity of introducing change into this kind of setting, managers should avoid the temptation to think, – 'This seems a good idea; let's try it and see how we get on'. Such an approach will lead to increased stress for staff and bad decisions being made. Instead, a basic exercise in stock-taking is probably the best way to proceed. Which drinkers to focus on, with what strategies, how to train counsellors, and most important, how should decisions be made within the team, are all questions which are best addressed in the form of a workshop or a period of time-out from normal routine. Using an independent consultant is often the best way to proceed.

Planning involves a number of stages. Identifying the aims and objectives of the hostel is one of the first issues to get agreement on; so too, one of the early tasks is to estimate the size of the potential client group, something which can be done in an average health district (see Orford 1987). It will also be useful to note the range of strategies which could be used with clients at different stages of change. Other key elements in the planning process, and the crucial issue of how to go about making these important decisions about priorities, can be found in Gawlinski and Graessle's (1988) self-help book on planning. Whatever the outcome of this process, it is always advisable to review progress on a regular basis.

Precisely what comes out of this kind of self-evaluation will vary from one setting to another. The challenge facing staff and managers is to find a balance between maintaining a workable hostel routine on the one hand, and developing an individualized approach to treatment on the other.

What goals should clients pursue?

If hostel programmes should adjust to clients and not the other way around, and if clients enter this environment at all stages of change, what goals should be pursued with them? The obvious solution is to plan a thorough intake assessment with all clients before or soon after admission in order to establish what they need and what they want.

An issue which often arises is whether asylum or drinking reform should be the main function of admission. Put in another way, clients are frequently referred who are pre-contemplators in terms of their substance use, but who are in need of asylum because they are homeless, in poor health, and so on; little thought has been given, as yet, to the possibility of changing drinking behaviour. Hostels need to make a policy decision about the acceptability of this kind of referral, and not leave this sometimes confusing issue for the intake interviewer to resolve. In principle it should be possible to offer such people the asylum they need as well as the opportunity to address the possibility of a change in drinking behaviour. In practice, this can be difficult because it considerably enlarges the potential pool of clients who could use the hostel, and because it raises the possibility of drinking on or off the hostel premises, an issue to be discussed in more detail in the next section. However this is resolved, clients should not be made to feel inadequate or unmotivated if drinking reform is not their highest priority.

The stages of change framework implies that multiple goals can be pursued with an individual client, and that some clients will have different goals from others. Exploring ambivalence about drinking, understanding dependence and withdrawal, making a choice between abstinence and controlled drinking goals, coping with family conflict, learning to assert oneself in specific situations, looking for a job, joining clubs, finding a flat – these are all goals which could be identified soon after admission. Adopting this kind of individualized approach does not mean, however, that programme organization within the hostel should descend into a confusing and complex array of individually tailored mini-programmes. Some clients will no doubt benefit from attending a single group which focuses on a particular topic, for example how to cope with pubs, clubs and drinking situations. Variability in programme content need not be a problem, as long as it is clear which programme is tailored to which stage of change, and where in this framework the client is found.

It is important to note that the goals set for clients should not merely entail attending this or that meeting, or undergoing this or that psychological change while resident in the hostel. Using the stages of change framework implies a fundamental shift in the programme orientation: residents and staff should be focused on the 'outside world' in which the individual's problems arose in the first place. Exposure to 'cues' like family, friends, landlords, drinking situations, and job centres should take place as part of routine care. This will be the best way to ensure that change is maintained and relapse is prevented.

Finally, one goal of residential care that is often overlooked is the provision of temporary respite care for those at the maintenance stage. Clients who have a long history of dependence may do better if they are able to seek regular brief stays in order to limit the damage threatened by drinking incidents. Another variant of this strategy already in existence in some centres is the managed flats system for those at the maintenance stage.

What should be done about drinking on the premises?

It is not uncommon for hostel staff to give breath tests to clients to see whether or not they have been drinking. This practice is consistent with the disease-oriented model of treatment used in most hostels. Prospective clients usually need to be abstinent for anything from six weeks to one day before admission, and drinking among residents is not permitted either on or off the premises. Breath-testing can give rise to conflict because clients are often unable to meet these expectations.

It is important to note that these drinking rules are incompatible with the use of a stages of change model. To require applicants for admission to be abstinent beforehand is to make an assumption that they should be at the action stage, when we know that they appear at all stages of change; some will not be ready to change their behaviour. One could argue, for example, that commitment to change is more likely to develop on the platform of stable accommodation, and that it is more important to facilitate admission than to construct a major obstacle for clients and referrers which, if clients could meet it, might question the need for residential treatment in the first place. Given the role of alcohol to aid coping with new situations, both threatening and unpredictable, it might be considered not unreasonable for new arrivals to ease their way to the front door with a little morale-booster. The basic point being made here is hostels must be capable of offering help to clients at all stages of change.

The rule about drinking once a client has been admitted to the hostel is also vulnerable to the same criticism; although it can serve to strengthen coherence and harmony and allow for the easier management of the tensions in the hot-house atmosphere of hostel settings, it is also incompatible with the stages of change framework. Increasingly, services eager to promote good practice will need to consider not only clients having differing drinking goals but also that exposure to alcohol for some clients will be an appropriate behavioural treatment.

To argue that the drinking rule might need to be abolished does not mean that clients should be free to drink whenever they like. Clearly a new set of more subtle and individual tailored rules would need to be established. It would be naive to suggest that operating such a flexible system will be an easy matter for staff and clients. However, this challenge might have to be faced if hostels are to provide the kind of help described in the first part of this book.

Conclusions

Two broad conclusions have emerged from this overview of different settings. First a pre-contemplator in a general practice setting is different from a pre-contemplator in a residential setting, and so on for drinkers at other stages. Therefore, we cannot generalize about the needs of drinkers at different stages without taking into account the setting in which they are found. When we do this, we find that a number of setting-specific issues arise. How do you train volunteers in an alcohol advice centre to work in the community with drinkers at the maintenance and relapse stages? What should the general practitioner do about pre-contemplators who don't have alcohol-related problems and who don't think they drink too much? How do residential workers deal with the new client, a contemplator, who says she still needs a drink but has serious social problems and needs support? These issues need to be tackled if the stages of change framework is to be truly useful. Second, using the stages of change framework implies greater flexibility in service design; this implies change, and change can be difficult for service providers to initiate and maintain, just as it is for the clients themselves; but it should be worth the effort.

Acknowledgements

The authors wish to acknowledge the feedback received from Nick Heather, Alison Bell and Jennifer Tebbit. This chapter was written while Stephen Rollnick was a Visiting Research Fellow at the National Drug and Alcohol Research Centre, University of New South Wales, Sydney, Australia.

References

Anderson, P. (1987) 'Early intervention in general practice', in S. Clement and T. Stockwell (eds) *Helping the Problem Drinker: New Initiatives in Community Care*, London: Croom Helm.

Chick, J., Lloyd, G. and Crombie, E. (1985) 'Counselling problem drinkers in medical wards', *British Medical Journal*, 290: 965–7.

Clement, S. (1987) 'The Salford experiment: an account of the community alcohol team approach', in S. Clement and T. Stockwell (eds) *Helping the Problem Drinker: New Initiatives in Community Care*, London: Croom Helm.

Gawlinski, G. and Graessle, L. (1988) *Planning Together: The Art of Effective Teamwork*, London: Bedford Square Press.

Heather, N. (1987) 'DRAMS for problem drinkers: the potential of a brief intervention by general practitioners and some evidence of its effectiveness', in S. Clement and T. Stockwell (eds) *Helping the Problem Drinker: New Initiatives in Community Care*, London: Croom Helm.

—— (1989) 'Psychology and brief interventions', *British Journal of Addiction* 84: 357–70.

Heather, N. and Robertson, I. (1985) *Problem Drinking: The New Approach*, Harmondsworth: Penguin.

Kristenson, H., Ohlin, H., Bulten-Nosslin, M., Trell, E. and Hood, B. (1983) 'Identification and intervention of heavy drinking in middle-aged men: results and follow-up', *Journal of Alcohol Clinical and Experimental Research* 20: 203–9.

Miller, W.R. (1983) 'Motivational interviewing with problem drinkers', *Behavioural Psychotherapy* 11: 147–72.

Miller, W.R. and Rollnick, S. (in preparation) *Motivational Interviewing: Preparing People for Change*.

Orford, J. (1987) 'The need for a community response to alcohol-related problems', in S. Clement and T. Stockwell (eds) *Helping the Problem Drinker: New Initiatives in Community Care*, London: Croom Helm.

Rollnick, S. (1985) 'The value of a cognitive-behavioural approach in the treatment of problem drinkers', in N. Heather, I. Robertson and P. Davies (eds) *The Misuse of Alcohol: Crucial Issues in Dependence Treatment and Prevention*, London: Croom Helm.

—— (1987) 'Early intervention among excessive drinkers: how early and in what context?' *Australian Drug and Alcohol Review* 6: 341–6.

Russell, M., Wilson, C., Taylor, C. and Baker, C. (1979) 'Effect of general practitioners' advice against smoking', *British Medical Journal* 231–5.

Stott, N.C.H. and Pill, R.M. (1988) *Health Checks in General Practice*, Cardiff, University of Wales, College of Medicine.

Thom, B. and Tellez, C. (1986) 'A difficult business: detecting and managing alcohol problems in general practice', *British Journal of Addiction* 81: 405–18.

Wallace, P., Cutler, S. and Haines, A. (1988) 'Randomized controlled trial of general practitioner intervention in patients with excessive alcohol consumption', *British Medical Journal* 297: 663–8.

Chapter seven

Motivational counselling in groups

Ken Barrie

Introduction

The use of groups is an established method of intervention for helping people who are experiencing problems in various aspects of their life. Some people experience problems related to their drinking and the use of group approaches can be an effective way of helping them to reduce their problems and change their drinking behaviour. This chapter outlines the historical use of groupwork in helping people with alcohol problems, the aims of groups and selection of group membership. In addition, methods which have been shown to be effective are outlined and a timetable for a group approach based on stages in the process of change (Prochaska and DiClemente 1983) is presented.

The benefits of groupwork have been written about at length elsewhere (Douglas 1976); nevertheless it is worth while to consider the positive aspects of this approach for those with alcohol problems.

Groups and problem drinkers: background

Groupwork has been a popular method of intervention for using with people who have problems, particularly since the Second World War. The increase in the use of such approaches and their popularity sprang, in part, from economic necessity in that helping agencies were aware of an increasing number of people making demands on their services without the increase in staff required to sustain the same level of individual interventions.

Around the same time social psychologists found that people's behaviour in a group was likely to be greatly influenced by that setting. Certain behaviours could be increased and skills enhanced, while certain other behaviours could decrease and performance deteriorate. Thus research findings gave credibility to the new and developing methods of intervention which fall under the title of groupwork.

Perhaps surprisingly the idea of people with similar problems meeting to discuss with one another and support one another had been established for a considerable time amongst people with alcohol problems. Alcoholics Anonymous originated in the USA in the mid-1930s in the social context of the ending of prohibition of alcohol in that country (Heather and Robertson 1985). Once established in the USA these self-help groups flourished and now estimates would suggest that worldwide membership is in excess of 1 million people.

As discussed in Chapter 1 the main aim of the AA meetings is to encourage sharing, whereby individuals identify with one another on the basis of having difficulties in common, namely 'alcoholism'. This is achieved by people telling the story of their problem-drinking history, thus enabling individuals to share their experiences with the rest of the group and also for the group to identify with the problem. Robinson (1979) identified that AA members found talks, stories and discussions to be the most helpful aspects of AA attendance over and above business and administrative matters. Active involvement in AA is encouraged and through time individuals' experience of AA will change from initially seeking support for their own sobriety to helping others. Thus AA becomes a way of life not only in terms of length of involvement over time but also in terms of having an impact on other spheres of the individual's life (Alcoholics Anonymous 1955).

Alcoholics Anonymous has been central to the development of a whole range of self-help groups for people experiencing similar difficulties, unrelated to the use of alcohol. Apart from its impact on responses to social problems its influence on our understanding of alcohol problems and the way in which helping services have responded has been profound.

Indeed when statutory and non-statutory organizations for alcohol problems began to develop in the 1960s, AA's influence was strongly felt in that clients would be advised about their 'illness' and group interventions would often be very similar to an Alcoholics Anonymous meeting. Many of the helpers, particularly in the emerging non-statutory sector, were active or former AA members. Therefore the AA approach and style of group intervention spread and developed in new areas of service delivery. It is possible that the extent of AA's influence resulted in the belief that problem drinkers got help only in groups, thus perhaps reinforcing some helpers' belief that they did not have the appropriate skills to help this client group effectively.

The AA approach to 'alcoholism' involves a particular style of group approach but in addition, it involves the promulgation of a belief system about alcohol problems and a way of life which may maintain sobriety for some problem drinkers. Not all people with alcohol problems will use AA nor will all who attend maintain lifelong contact. As a consequence a wide range of styles of groupwork are likely to be appropriate with regard to helping problem drinkers.

What groupwork has to offer the problem drinker

Problem drinkers are likely to benefit in much the same way as other people with problems do in group situations. While there is a great debate in the addiction field as to the effectiveness of intervention or treatment (see Chapter 1), it has been suggested with regard to groupwork that 'this type of therapy appears to be less costly than individual treatment in terms of staff and money. Almost all research has shown that group therapy is at least as effective as, and less expensive than, individual treatment' (Rose 1986: 443–4).

Apart from equivalent effectiveness in terms of 'outcome' and cost-effectiveness relative to individual methods there are a number of other benefits to be gained from the group situation.

1 The experience of being in a group is central to human existence. Given that attitudes and behaviour are largely formed in a group setting they should also be amenable to change in a similar setting.
2 A group setting is likely to offer problem drinkers the opportunity to see that they are not alone in their difficulties. This is particularly important, as those who develop a drink problem are likely to be stigmatized by family and community alike.
3 The group offers its members a unique opportunity to practise and develop new interactive behaviours in a protected setting.
4 The opportunity is offered to enable members to give and receive both positive and negative feedback with regard to attitudes and behaviour. In addition feedback from peers is likely to be more acceptable than from the group leader; thus the distinctions between helper and helped are less clear.
5 Given the development of a range of norms created by the group the imposition by the group leader of their values becomes less easy. A group is more likely than individuals to challenge or disagree with the counsellor's or helper's values and opinions without detriment.

6 By giving feedback to others, individual group members become helpers in their own right. This is of great importance in increasing individuals' beliefs in their own abilities and is important in terms of maintaining any well-being gained after the group finishes. Such opportunities also take the focus away from the group leader as the only available helper.

7 The opportunity to give feedback or to reinforce the attitudes and behaviour of others in the group is important within the group and may be generalized to the members' functioning in other social settings. It has been suggested that as individuals learn to reinforce others they are reciprocally reinforced by others. As a consequence mutual approval and liking will increase, as well as group cohesion (Rose 1986).

8 As interaction within the group develops members are involved in the creation of and adherence to a range of uniquely created norms. These norms should function to enhance the initial or agreed aims of the group and, in fact, it is the group leader's task to ensure that this happens. Such norms are powerful and the group will influence members who deviate from the rules to conform, for example attendance, forcefulness of feedback, drinking between meetings (if appropriate), arriving intoxicated, abstinence.

9 The group setting may also offer the opportunity for a more complete assessment of the individual's situation, as members can be observed interacting with other people.

10 People are often vague about the exact nature of their difficulties even with regard to drinking. The group setting may offer members the opportunity to identify their problems more clearly and in so doing develop their own self-assessment skills as well as moving towards resolution of their difficulties.

11 The group setting can also be used to teach new behaviours and skills. In this context the group offers individual members a wide range of persons who can be used as 'role models'. It also provides the opportunity for role-playing and behavioural rehearsal. In such a setting the members have the opportunity to practise behaviours which have been identified as potential solutions to problems.

12 Group members may also be used as partners in homework tasks which have been agreed between meetings.

13 The group setting provides the forum for reporting back and monitoring behaviour and measuring the achievement of agreed tasks between meetings, but additionally offers the opportunity of assessing change on the basis of individual's performance in the group.

14 The opportunity is provided to anticipate and effectively prevent difficult and stressful situations which may invite a return
to problem-drinking levels. Thus the prevention and management of problems or relapse becomes possible.

Some or all of these beneficial aspects of groupwork with problem
drinkers will be brought into play depending largely on the aims
and structure of the group. Behavioural approaches to groups can
be looked upon as a continuum from short-term intervention
involving training to intensive long-term therapy (Rose 1977). At
the 'training' end of the continuum, groups focus on the teaching
and development of specific skills. As a result of this and the limited
number of sessions involved, a specific agenda is used in each of the
group meetings, thus allowing only a limited range of flexibility. At
the more intensive end of the continuum a wide range of intervention methods are used and the group is able to focus more on the
situation of the individuals. With the increase in time and the
flexibility in the nature of the group the influence of group
processes and norms become more important, and powerful, as
therapeutic devices.

Groupwork aims and methods appropriate to the model of change

Almost all helping strategies are based on the assumption that
individuals wish to change something about their situation in order
to minimize negative consequences of their behaviour. Despite this
it is not uncommon for those who come into contact with 'problem
drinkers' to find that some people do not appear to want to change
their drinking behaviour, while some of those who do stop or cut
down return to their previous pattern of problem drinking rather
sooner than was hoped for. The first part of this book demonstrated that people with drug and alcohol problems may fall into
different stages in the process of change. It was suggested that
problem drinkers are likely to think and act differently, depending
on their preparedness to change. Consideration of these stages of
change will help identify which individuals might be prepared to
change their beliefs or drinking behaviour. By implication the
appropriate strategies which may be employed in a group can be
identified as well as clarifying what sort of group might be suitable
to an individual.

Matching the stages of change with a group approach

Pre-contemplation stage

Pre-contemplators are those who use the least change strategies. The nature of the pre-contemplation stage was discussed in Chapter 2; such individuals have traditionally been seen as having problems of denial or lack of motivation. Nevertheless they may well be in contact with an agency in relation to health, child care, legal or employment problems; as a consequence they may be suitable group members. The group setting may offer clients an opportunity to re-assess their situation and consider the extent to which alcohol plays a part in their difficulties, whether social, health or legal.

As pre-contemplators are unlikely to change their drinking behaviour because of its perceived benefits, there are a number of aims which may be tackled in the group setting (see Table 7.1).

First, the opportunity is given to offer information on the impact of alcohol on the drinker's health, and of the social and legal consequences related to drinking. Second, given that drinking behaviour is likely to continue, the next aim is to enable individuals to examine their health and social situation thus reducing or limiting the harm which might accrue through continued drinking. The third aim is to attempt to alter the client's motivation by identifying reasons for drinking and the links between that behaviour and any difficulties or life events which may have been experienced (e.g. court appearances, health problems, reception into care of a child). It may be more appropriate to deal with pre-contemplators in a group by themselves. Care should be taken when including them in a group with those at the 'contemplation' and 'action' stages, because pre-contemplators may influence such a group negatively by disagreeing that alcohol is a problem and that change may be required.

Contemplation stage

Contemplators are those at the stage in the process of change who are considering the need to do something about their drinking (see Chapter 3). They will currently be using alcohol, perhaps quite heavily, but will be dissatisfied with that situation. They are likely to look for information about alcohol (e.g. posters or pamphlets) and are likely to feel that their reliance on alcohol makes them disappointed in themselves, although they may experience conflict between the positive and negative aspects of their drinking.

Contemplators may not yet be ready to change their behaviour but they are ready to absorb information, raise their consciousness

Table 7.1 Pre-contemplation stage change strategies, group aims and
        methods

Change strategies
  1 Benefits of alcohol use perceived rather than the costs
  2 May see things other than alcohol as problematic
  3 Use fewer 'change' strategies than others
  4 May avoid 'help' and information
Groupwork aims
  1 Provide information on alcohol and related problems
  2 Give opportunity to identify problems and make links to alcohol
     consumption
  3 Presume continued alcohol use amongst membership and emphasize harm
     reduction and health maintenance
Group methods
  1 Information giving
  2 Cost-benefit exercise
  3 Involvement in identifying harm-reduction methods appropriate to the
     individual
  4 Opportunity to cease contact or seek help appropriate to stage in process of
     change at which individuals find themselves

Table 7.2 Contemplation stage change strategies, group aims and methods

---

Change strategies
  1 Consciousness-raising
  2 Self-re-evaluation in relation to alcohol use
  3 Looking for information on alcohol problems and help available
Groupwork aims
  1 To raise consciousness about alcohol-related problems
  2 To increase commitment toward changing drinking behaviour
Group methods
  1 Provision of information on health and social consequences
  2 Record and monitor drinking behaviour by using a drinking diary
  3 Identify problems and facilitate the expression of concern
  4 Advice on the nature of help available

---

about their drinking and change their attitudes and beliefs about
both themselves and drinking. The broad aims of a groupwork
intervention for contemplators would consist of, first, providing
information on alcohol and related problems as well as advising on
the type and range of help available and what such help consists of.
Second, by identifying problems which individuals experience in
relation to their drinking and considering the costs and benefits of
continued or changed drinking behaviour, the aim is to increase
individuals' perception or belief that there is a need to change their
behaviour (see Table 7.2).

Ken Barrie

Table 7.3 Action stage change strategies, group aims and methods

---

Change strategies
  1 Self-re-evaluation in relation to alcohol use
  2 Self-liberation or 'I can do it if I want to'
  3 Use of a helping relationship
  4 Being rewarded by others for harm-free alcohol use
  5 Taking up alternative activities to help relaxation
Groupwork aims
  1 Maintain and enhance commitment to changing drinking behaviour
  2 Facilitate behaviour change
  3 Teach strategies to prevent and manage a breakdown of the resolution to change behaviour
Group methods
  1 Identify problems
  2 Facilitate the expression of concern by members
  3 Enhance the perception of the need to change
  4 Teach problem-solving techniques
  5 Identify benefits of change
  6 Identify harm-free activities

Action stage

Individuals in the action stage use the greatest number of change strategies. In a very real sense they are changing their opinions and beliefs about themselves. Individuals at this stage will tell themselves that they can succeed at changing their drinking. They are also likely to find it very useful having others who will support them in their continued behaviour change and in whom they can confide, such as fellow group members. They are also likely to have arranged to take up alternative activities instead of drinking when they want to relax or wind down. Self-help groups like Alcoholics Anonymous may be useful to some at this stage.

The aims of a group designed to respond to those in the action stage will include maintaining and increasing individuals' commitment to their changed behaviour, and developing strategies to help participants change their behaviour (e.g. problem-solving and goal-setting). Implicit in this approach is the need to develop relapse-prevention strategies, that is maintaining changed behaviour. In addition, however, it is important to prepare for the possibility of relapse and in this sense management of a relapse is an important aim (see Table 7.3). Similar intervention strategies aimed at the individual have been discussed in Chapter 4 and 5.

Maintenance stage

Individuals at the maintenance stage will have changed their drinking behaviour for quite some time, perhaps months or even

122

Table 7.4 Maintenance stage change strategies, group aims and methods

---

Change strategies
  1 Removing things or self from the environment which remind
  2 Engage in activities other than drinking to relax
Groupwork aims
  1 Maintain changed behaviour
  2 Prevent and manage relapse
  3 Encourage general life-style change
Group methods
  1 Explore reasons for having changed drinking and reinforce them
  2 Consider benefits of harm-free drinking
  3 Encourage vigilance over risky situations
  4 Encourage the development of activities to replace harmful drinking

---

years. Despite this they still use change strategies to maintain their harm-free drinking (see Chapter 5). They are still likely to be vigilant in situations which can be difficult, such as meeting old drinking friends, and will actively remove things from their physical or social environment which remind them of the problematic behaviour. Like people at the action stage, they will engage in alternative activities to drinking heavily when they wish to relax or socialize.

The main aims of a groupwork response for individuals at this stage would be first, to maintain commitment to the changed behaviour or way of life, and by implication prevent relapse. Focusing much less on drinking behaviour means that an overall life-style change is a major aim in a group for people at this stage; by taking up new activities and changing relationships, they are creating a new way of life (see Table 7.4). Such groups may be more open-ended as opposed to time limited. Attendance at Alcoholics Anonymous meetings may fulfil these aims for some people not only in that abstinence may be maintained but also by offering a new way of life to some of its members.

Relapse stage

Individuals at the relapse stage or where their resolutions have broken down (see Chapter 5) also use change strategies. Despite the conventional wisdom of relapse being seen as a failure or being 'back to square one', this is not the case, in that individuals use a range of change strategies which are a combination of those used in contemplation and action (Prochaska and DiClemente 1983). This means that relapse is very much an active part of the process of change and is consequently an appropriate focus for a groupwork approach. The main aims of such a group would be a combination of those used in both contemplation and action, the aim being to move individuals from thinking about changing their drinking behaviour to doing something about it, as well as to help them prevent and manage any future return to harmful drinking.

A group programme for those who wish to change their drinking behaviour

As we have seen, not all people who experience problems from their drinking wish to change their drinking behaviour. Those who do, regardless of the extent or severity of their problems, have usually come to perceive the benefits of drinking as being outweighed by the costs (Saunders and Allsop 1986).

Two major problems then face a group who have come together to change their drinking behaviour. The first is to maintain and enhance the belief that the extent of the problems and the concern felt about them warrants some sort of action. This may be achieved by participants being enabled to outline their own perception of their difficulties and to express their concerns about these problems, rather than simply being told what needs to be done by the group leader. In this sense 'a person is more likely to integrate and accept that which is reached by his or her own reasoning processes' (Miller 1983: 160).

The second problem area is that, even if group participants' commitment to change remains high, how do they then cope with the wide range of difficult situations and emotions which will present themselves and would normally have been 'solved' by drinking? In other words, how might relapse or failure of resolution be prevented?

Given the high 'failure of resolution' amongst problem drinkers the fact that participants are likely to drink at some future date needs to be built into such a programme. Given the myriad of potentially 'dangerous' situations for an individual, let alone a group, it is not possible to teach individual skills for every single risky situation. What is possible, however, is to teach problem-solving skills which can be generalized, that is, once they have been learnt they can be applied to a wide range of problematic situations (D'Zurilla and Goldfried 1971). Indeed it has been suggested that problem drinkers are poor problem-solvers (Heather and Robertson 1985). Billings and Moos (1983) indicate that two years after formal treatment one of the major contrasts between survivors and relapsers was the extent to which problem-solving and coping skills were employed.

In essence then, the process of change model would suggest that a group intent on changing drinking behaviour needs to have the opportunity to maintain and enhance their resolution to change as well as learn and practise new methods which may reduce the risk of a return to harmful drinking. As a consequence of these needs the group leader must be a facilitator, educator, director and supporter of change. The need for members to make active use of the group experience outside that setting is emphasized. It has been noted that 'performance based interventions more readily achieve both behaviour and attitude change than do purely verbal procedures, in other words the problem drinker should have practice in doing the things necessary for a change in lifestyle' (Rollnick 1985: 140).

A groupwork blueprint

In this section the theoretical issues raised earlier in this chapter and elsewhere in the book are applied in the group setting. A blueprint group timetable has been designed to be implemented in five sessions lasting about two to two and a half hours for about four or five participants. The structure is flexible and it may be appropriate to spend longer on certain aspects of the programme. The format can be adapted according to the stage of change of the participants and in this sense the content of sessions one and two would be appropriate for a group of contemplators, while those at the action stage would require an emphasis on relapse prevention. The overall themes of the group programme are those of behavioural and problem-solving techniques.

Objectives

1 to help identify problems related to drinking
2 to maintain and enhance a commitment to change drinking behaviour
3 to teach methods of resolving drinking problems
4 to monitor behaviour
5 to prevent a return to problem drinking
6 to help cope with a lapse.

Session one

The main task of this session, apart from making people feel comfortable and welcome, is to focus on people's concerns about their drinking problems. By identifying their problems and expressing concern it is likely that individuals' 'commitment to change' or motivation will be enhanced. By implication the perception of a need to change drinking behaviour will be clearer. It will be appropriate in some instances to split the group into small discussion groups of two or three to maximize the opportunity for individuals to talk about their concerns. The following topics should be covered.

1 Discussion on individuals' expectations of the group. Clarification of some basic rules, e.g. turning up sober.
2 What problems are experienced in relation to drinking? Encourage participants to identify the problems which they experience in relation to alcohol. An emphasis should be placed on describing problematic drinking in its social context and identifying the positive and negative consequences, e.g. What is the problem? Where does it happen? When does it happen? Whom does it affect?
3 Allow participants to express their concern about their problems.
4 Participants should be enabled to consider the costs and benefits of their drinking behaviour. On the basis of such an analysis, individuals who decide that change is necessary will be supported by the group.
5 Homework task: ask the participants to identify a situation which is likely to result in their starting to drink.

Session two

This session is concerned with participants discussing situations which are likely to result in their drinking heavily and also looking at the consequences. Problem-solving skills should be taught in order that participants may develop skills which will enable them to change their behaviour and break the link between difficult situations or feelings, drinking and harmful consequences. The following topics should be covered.

1 Feedback from group regarding the 'homework' from the last session. Participants should be encouraged to identify situations which precede heavy drinking. As such they may be defined as risky or problematic situations. The link between risky situations or negative emotions and subsequent drinking and problems should be emphasized.
2 Teach problem-solving techniques in line with the procedure described on p. 127.
3 Enable the group to rehearse problem-solving skills by using each individual's high-risk situation. Such 'risk' situations could

include emotions, conflict with partners or being offered drinks by friends. By following this procedure participants should have a range of potential solutions, other than drinking, to a specific problematic situation.

4 Participants should have the opportunity to rehearse the behaviour which has been identified as a potential solution.

5 Homework task: to use problem-solving skills and carry out the solutions or goals which were decided upon.

Problem-solving skills

Rationale

Making decisions is a general part of life and a problem-solving difficulty exists when an individual has no effective response to a specific situation.

Orientation

Problems are viewed as things to be solved, not a confused mess over which the individual has no influence. Problem-solving is a technique which can be learned.

Definition

It is essential that a client's 'problems' are clearly defined. 'My marriage is a mess' is not soluble, but 'My spouse objects to the time I spend at work' may have a solution. Precise definition followed by 'prioritizing' is necessary.

Generation of solutions

What are the possible solutions to each specific problem? Brainstorm without criticism, indeed the more wild the ideas the better as this often generates novel solutions. The focus is on quantity of potential solutions resulting in more high-quality solutions.

Decision-making

Which of the possible solutions are attractive to the client? Which does the client wish to pursue? The pros and cons of each potential solution may need to be considered.

Verification

Assessment of chosen solutions either by 'thinking through' or carrying out the behaviour to determine whether a solution is likely to be effective.

Ken Barrie

Session three

This session will consist of identifying the extent to which participants have used the problem-solving skills and how useful this was in terms of identifying solutions and achieving goals which were decided upon. Participants should be encouraged to rehearse problem-solving methods again within the group and rehearse behaviours which have been identified as potential solutions or goals. Problem-solving may also be used effectively to resolve interactional difficulties within the group which adversely influence the therapeutic aim of the group. The following topics should be covered.

1 Feedback from the participants regarding their attempts to use problem-solving skills and achieve goals set.
2 Were goals achieved fully, in part or not at all? If the goals were achieved then the participant should receive reinforcement from the rest of the group. If the goal was not achieved then it is important to identify the barriers to success.
3 Rehearsal of specific goal-achieving behaviours should be encouraged.
4 Homework task: carry out specific goal-oriented behaviour.

Session four

Once again participants' efforts and achievements should be reviewed since the last meeting. Given the high likelihood of participants drinking, perhaps problematically at some future date, the approaches already taught should now focus on managing a return to problematic drinking rather than trying to prevent it. No attempt should be made to reinforce the notion that heavy drinking is acceptable but that it is likely to occur and will be worth being prepared for, thus preventing a few drinks developing into problematic drinking. The following topics should be covered.

1 Feedback from participants regarding homework from the previous session. Use of problem-solving technique if there is an identified problem in relation to goal achievement.
2 The possibility of drinking in the future should be introduced and participants' views on the consequences sought. Some resistance can be expected in raising this subject, particularly if participants are committed to abstinence.
3 The focus of the group's concern should be on how harmful effects might be minimized. In this context a problem-solving

approach would be appropriate. Participants may wish to take notes to which they can refer in the future.

4 Homework task: to negotiate with friends or relatives what sort of help and support they may be able to offer, should drinking become problematic.

Session five

The main function of this session is to review the participants' progress and identify what they require next. Such a review should involve recapping on their perceived need for change in their drinking behaviour, thereby maintaining and enhancing the need to change behaviour or to maintain and build on achievements already made. The following topics should be covered.

1 Feedback from homework agreed in the previous session.
2 Recap on reasons for wishing to change behaviour. Participants should be enabled to reflect on their reasons for wishing to change in the group's first session and the extent to which they have achieved their aims.
3 On the basis of this discussion the future of the group, if any, or its membership can be agreed. Some may feel the need to continue meeting while others may consider that they require something different in order to maintain and develop their situation.

Evaluation

Several types of evaluation of a group may be necessary. First, individual group members will require to evaluate their own degree of change as a consequence of the group process. This is separate from the individual's evaluation of this group as a whole. The group facilitator should also be in a position to evaluate the group with regard to the extent to which initial group aims have been achieved. In this sense a successful group for pre-contemplators may mean that some of the membership have moved toward thinking about their drinking while a successful group for the action stage may be related to the extent of harm-free drinking.

Difficulties can arise in the group setting when participants' aims and needs are widely divergent. This is often a consequence of mixing people who are at very different stages in the process of changing. Individuals who think that their drinking is not a problem may feel threatened and behave in a disruptive manner in a group where the majority have decided to change their drinking behaviour. Similarly the group might feel threatened in that such people may be perceived as not trying or undermining their good efforts. Given that individuals may be at different stages in the process of change the group interventions should address a particular stage rather than take everyone. Having said this, relapsers tend to think and act in similar ways to those at the contemplation and action stages and in such instances the possibility of 'mixing' becomes more feasible and helpful to participants.

Conclusion

To conclude then, the use of groups for problem drinkers as well as other people experiencing difficulties is well established. Groupwork may offer a cost-effective method of responding to some problem drinkers who are in contact with helping agencies, often in considerable numbers. Similarly individual drinkers' preparedness to change will enable them to become members of an appropriate group with aims coinciding with their needs. A wide range of tested and effective intervention strategies may be used in the group setting, thus enhancing the already powerful impact of group norms and processes on an individual's behaviour.

References

Alcoholics Anonymous (1955) *Alcoholics Anonymous*, 2nd edn, New York: Alcoholics Anonymous World Services.

Billings, A. and Moos, R. (1983) 'Psychosocial processes of recovery among alcoholics and their families: implications for clinicians and programme evaluators', *Addictive Behaviours* 8: 205–18.

Douglas, T. (1976) *Groupwork Practice*, London: Tavistock.

D'Zurilla, T. and Goldfried, M. (1971) 'Problem solving and behaviour modification', *Journal of Abnormal Psychology* 78: 107–26.

Heather, N. and Robertson, I. (1985) *Problem Drinking: The New Approach*, Harmondsworth: Penguin.

Miller, W.R. (1983) 'Motivational interviewing with problem drinkers', *Behavioural Psychotherapy* 11: 147–72.

Prochaska, J.O. and DiClemente, C.C. (1983) 'Stages and processes of self change of smoking, towards an integrative model of change', *Journal of Consulting and Clinical Psychology* 51: 390–5.

Robinson, D. (1979) *Talking Out of Alcoholism: The Self-Help Process of Alcoholics Anonymous*, London: Croom Helm.

Rollnick, S. (1985) 'The value of a cognitive-behavioural approach in the treatment of problem drinkers', in N. Heather, I. Robertson and P. Davies (eds) *The Misuse of Alcohol: Crucial Issues in Dependence,*

Treatment and Prevention, London: Croom Helm.

Rose, S.D. (1977) *Group Therapy: Behavioural Approach*, Englewood Cliffs, NJ: Prentice-Hall.

—— (1986) 'Group methods', in F. Kanfer and A. Goldstein (eds) *Helping People Change: A Textbook of Methods*, 3rd edn, New York: Pergamon.

Saunders, B. (1985) 'Treatment doesn't work: some criteria of failure', in N. Heather, I. Robertson, and P. Davies (eds) *The Misuse of Alcohol: Crucial Issues in Dependence, Treatment and Prevention*, London: Croom Helm.

Saunders, B. and Allsop, S. (1986) 'Giving up addiction', in F. Watts (ed.) *New Developments in Clinical Psychology*, Chichester: John Wiley.

Saunders, B. and Allsop, S. (1987) 'Relapse: a psychological perspective', *British Journal of Addiction* 82, 4: 417–29.

Chapter eight

The influence of life events

Moyra Sidell

Introduction

The term 'life events' has inserted itself so firmly into our vocabulary that we scarcely stop to think what it means or why it has become so significant in recent years. The literal meaning simply entails all the things that happen to a person in the course of his or her life. Recent usage of the term is more precise. It implies that the individual is the object of a life event, not the subject or initiator; there is an element of chance, so that negative life events are bad luck or misfortune, positive life events are good luck or fortune. The trivial happenings of everyday life do not qualify for the epithet 'life event', and most attention is focused on negative or stressful life events which are thought to adversely affect the individual, although the individual does not necessarily effect them.

In the 1970s there was a proliferation of literature reifying the concept of life events and relating it to various illnesses and conditions (Dohrenwend and Dohrenwend 1974; Paykel *et al.* 1969; Holmes and Rahe 1967). The hypothesis implicit in most of the life events literature is that, under the impact of a certain number of stressful life events (such as bereavement, divorce, being made redundant), the organism succumbs to certain diseases or conditions such as heart disease or clinical depression. Life events research was mostly interested in negative life events and set out to quantify the life events experienced by people in a fixed period of time. Typically the events would be assigned a score in terms of perceived severity; a person could then be rated on a life events scale. The hypothesis was that pathology was associated with high scores. Brown and Harris (1978) developed a sophisticated model to explain the differential social class distribution of depression in women. The researchers investigated not only the impact of particular life events (which can be precisely fixed in time), but also long-term background difficulties (such as poverty or poor housing, and 'vulnerability' or 'protective' factors which might make a person more or less susceptible to the impact of stressful life events. Their work represents an attempt to bring a sociological dimension to the medical model of disease causation.

Life events and drinking behaviour

What relevance does this model have for understanding drinking behaviour? Clearly there are problems in relating such a model to alcohol use or misuse, the most obvious one being that it assumes a 'disease' model of 'alcoholism', that under the influence of stressful life events the individual will be a prey to the disease of alcoholism. But attempting to ascribe such a cause to what is in effect a behaviour is problematic. The search for *a* cause would seem to be a most unfruitful one, because the reasons why people become problem drinkers are likely to be many and varied, encompassing psychological and social factors in which life events may well play a part. What is possible and more useful is to look for associations between life events and drinking behaviour. The questions then to ask are how does a person react to stressful life events? Do some people react to stressful life events by drinking harmful amounts of alcohol and, if so, why? This approach is concerned with process. Counting events and ascribing a notional score to them is not relevant. What is required is to understand the context of the event and the meaning the event has had for the individual.

In an excellent review of life events research in the field of alcohol and drug addiction, O'Doherty and Davies (1987) discuss studies of the relationship between both originating problems and life events, and life events and relapses after intervention. They comment on various strengths and weaknesses of research of this type and criticize many studies, particularly when the studies rely on retrospective recall. They also draw attention to conceptual problems with the notion of life events, stressing the importance of the individual's perceptions of the life events, commenting that

> In most cases, cognitive processes will be important in determining the effects a particular event is likely to have on a given individual. A high degree of consensus about particular events does not have to exist, and the fact that it sometimes does should not be taken to imply that individual cognitive interpretations have no influence.
>
> (O'Doherty and Davies 1987: 133)

This leads O'Doherty and Davies to question the validity of the

Brown and Harris (1978) study, which used independent assessors to determine the degree of threat involved in a life event, irrespective of whether or not the individual in question felt threatened. A major difficulty with the concept of 'life event' for O'Doherty and Davies is that it is seen in isolation. A life event, they argue, is never context-free. They prefer to use the term 'life courses', defined as 'consisting of specific events at a "surface" level, which are interpreted as having significance (meaning?) at a deeper level' (1987: 135).

The 'life course' approach is much more akin to 'biographical' or 'life history' research, which attempts to understand human behaviour, not as caused by life events, but in the context of those events. In relation to drinking behaviour, it does not assume a disease model of alcohol abuse, but accepts that drinking behaviour might be influenced by these life events.

I have been involved in one such biographical study of fifty men and fifty women who had sought help at a community alcohol treatment centre for a drink problem (Fennell and Sidell 1989). This chapter draws on the experience gained in that study to look at the significance of life events/courses to a drinking career, before, during and after the treatment period and relates this to the stages identified by Prochaska and DiClemente (1984).

Life events and the misuse of alcohol

The debate as to whether there is a causal connection between stressful life events and the onset of problem drinking remains unresolved. Much of this debate focuses on women, who are considered by some to be particularly susceptible to alcohol abuse when faced with stressful life events (Beckman 1975). Others (Cooke and Allan 1984) disagree, claiming that the excessive stigma attached to women's drinking results in a need for a 'special explanation' which is provided by the evidence of stressful life events. Yet another view is that it is precisely the stigma attached to heavy drinking for women that has protected women in the past by discouraging them from heavy drinking. Therefore the use of alcohol for psychological relief is resorted to by women only at times of extreme stress.

The evidence from the study in which I was engaged is that, for slightly fewer than half of the people interviewed, stressful life events played a significant role in their subsequent alcohol consumption. This is not to say that the life events necessarily caused an increase in alcohol consumption, but only that some people reacted to stressful life events by increasing their alcohol consumption to harmful amounts. There seem to be two types: the first described themselves as regular social drinkers whose drinking escalated in reaction to a stressful life event; the second type had not been regular drinkers before the occurrence of a certain stressful life event, but they then responded to it by consuming alcohol. The distinction between the two groups is that, with the first group, their regular drinking could not in most cases be dissociated from the stressful life event, whereas with the second group, the event could not be associated with previous drinking. Significantly there were more men in the first group and more women in the second. The difference also reflects a qualitative difference in the life events. Certain life events could be identified as being independent of the condition being investigated, for example, bereavement, redundancy or retirement. Events, on the other hand, such as marital breakdown or dismissal from a job, could not be seen to be independent of the condition and might well be a consequence of it – they were in some way implicated.

Implicated life events

The events experienced by the first group in this study were not independent of their drinking behaviour and were predominantly to do with relationship breakdown and employment problems. In the case of employment problems, some people lost their jobs or failed to get promotion because of absenteeism or loss of concentration at work; this then precipitated their drinking into very heavy consumption. A typical sequence of events in the case of relationship breakdown would be where drinking caused friction within a relationship, resulting in the non-drinking spouse or partner leaving, whereupon the drinking partner would escalate his or her level of drinking. As one man explained:

> I was drinking more and more and the whole thing was just going to pieces, with me drinking and she wasn't drinking as much as I was. Eventually my wife found somebody else. She got fed up. She found somebody and she left and, of course, then the thing got worse because you're suddenly thrown in on your own. Weekends were always the worst when you're not at work and you would probably soldier through Saturday, probably start drinking Saturday afternoon and it gradually gets earlier and earlier and, in the end, because all you want to do is drink enough not to make yourself ill, but just enough to go and say, when I wake up, it's Sunday morning. That will be another day gone. Then Sunday lunchtime you start again because you've had

enough of Sunday but you've got to remember not to leave it too late because you've got to go to work on Monday.

Independent life events

The second smaller group, made up almost entirely of women who either did not drink at all, or only on ceremonial occasions, experienced life events which were independent of the drinking problem.

These events were mainly to do with sudden, unexpected and shocking bereavements. For some, it was the premature death of their partners; two women had lost teenage children. At the age of 26, another woman lost her sister with whom she had been very close, and another woman's mother died before she could reach her. As well as these bereavements, others experienced loss when their husbands deserted them. Many people, of course, lose loved ones in equally traumatic ways and do not seek to ease the pain with alcohol. Most of these women explained that it was not so much the loss which precipitated them into drinking alcohol, but the circumstances, and this was mostly to do with not having support through that loss. One woman explained her situation:

> I was just absolutely devastated and, at the time, the one person I thought I could turn to was my husband and he wasn't supportive. He used to tell me to pull myself together for my daughter's sake, but I just couldn't. Nobody wanted to listen, nobody wanted to know and you feel so terrible inside, there's nobody you can turn to. I seemed to just start it by, in the afternoon I'd have a couple of glasses of sherry and it used to make me feel sleepy and it was sort of cold and I just found that I would go to sleep and then I'd wake up, sort of time enough to pick my daughter up from school.

One young woman was raped, but it was her inability to talk about it which led her to resort to drink. She explained:

> When I was 17 I got raped on holiday abroad. I can't remember drinking much before then really. I think that made me much more scared of people. I felt unable to talk to people. I told my mother and she just burst into hysterics and so I just sort of kept it all in for ages and ages really. But then I used to get really pissed and then I'd go on telling people my life story and things like that. I couldn't talk about it without being drunk a lot of the time. I must have bored people in my first year at university because that was like about a year after it happened, you see.

Again, the circumstances surrounding the event were crucial.

Protective factors such as having the support of a loving and understanding relationship are clearly important when coping with stressful life events such as loss and bereavement. Thus life events should not be seen as isolated events but located within the social and psychological context in which they occur because this context will have an impact on how the individual reacts to and copes with these events. The need to support people through bereavement has become widely recognized in recent years with the setting up of counselling services to support people who may or may not have support or who need extra support. But we also need to be aware that as a society we freely advocate the use of alcohol in times of stress to 'drown the sorrows', 'relieve the tensions' or to 'seek oblivion'. And these messages are constantly reinforced in the media. It should therefore come as no surprise to us that some people react to stress by drinking harmful amounts of alcohol. A greater awareness is needed of the consequences of adopting what is considered a common and socially acceptable coping strategy.

If life events are associated with the onset of harmful drinking, how do they affect other aspects of a drinking career, such as the decision to seek help, and the subsequent treatment process?

Life events and the decision to seek help

Do life events play a part in moving someone from contemplation to action in the stages of change? A study (also cited in Chapter 1) helps to answer this question. Tuchfeld (1981) studied sixty-one problem drinkers who had remitted and found life events to be significant to that remission in two ways. The first was in provoking a commitment to change their drinking behaviour and the second was in maintaining that change. Tuchfeld's subjects did not seek treatment and so are said to have spontaneously remitted. It would seem that the same motivating force also operates to trigger other people into seeking help to change their behaviour. Some people may need little support, some people may have all the support they need from family and friends, but there is a group of people who feel the need for external help.

In our research we explored the process of seeking help with the fifty men and fifty women who had taken up treatment, and we paid particular attention to their reasons for seeking help when they did (Fennell and Sidell 1989). For many of them, life events did trigger the action to seek help. The life events which acted as triggers were not the independent-of-the-drinking-behaviour type, such as bereavement, but were more likely to be implicated in the drinking behaviour, and men were more likely to seek treatment triggered by some crisis event than women. There were mainly four types of crises events which acted as triggers.: domestic crises, physical events, traumatic incidents and employment/financial crises.

Domestic crises

There were two major types of domestic crises identified. One was the breakdown of a relationship where a spouse or partner left or threatened to leave because of the other partner's excessive drinking. The shock of this persuaded the drinker to seek help. The other was to do with domestic violence; either the violent reactions from partners because of the drinking, or because the drinkers found themselves capable of violent acts against their partners.

Physical events

These were mainly acute physical problems associated with heavy drinking. Some were severe, for example a stomach haemorrhage or acute liver failure. Some people experienced blackouts, and one had a fit, all of which were attributed to heavy drinking. But for others, it was the shock of being told that they had raised liver function tests which triggered them into seeking treatment. All these physical events or crises served to focus their minds on the harm that they were inflicting upon themselves and strengthened their resolve to seek help.

Traumatic incidents

These incidents mostly involved legal infringements, committing offences under the influence of alcohol, such as burglary or vandalism. Others got into fights when drunk and ended up in the courts. These mainly involved men. Women also had brushes with the law, for example shoplifting when drunk, or drunken behaviour in public places. A combination of shock at the occurrence of the event and strong advice from the probation or social services served to trigger them into treatment. Other than legal incidents, some suffered accidents when drunk, one woman falling down the stairs and ending up in the Accident and Emergency Department; one woman set fire to her bed and had to be hospitalized.

Employment/financial crises

Being warned at work that their drinking behaviour was adversely affecting their work triggered some people, both men and women, into seeking help. In the case of a nurse, her seeking treatment was a condition of retaining her job, and this acted as a powerful motivating force where previous advice had failed. Getting into financial difficulties was almost a universal experience of all the people interviewed but, surprisingly, only two sought help primarily because of financial problems. For them it was the shock of being in serious debt which prompted their decision to seek help.

Life events and stages of change

With the exception of legal problems, the events or crises which triggered some people into seeking help were precisely the same types of events or crises which precipitated others into further heavy drinking. Prochaska and DiClemente's model of stages of readiness to change provides us with a framework for understanding this. In the pre-contemplative stage when individuals have not thought about the consequences of harmful drinking, stressful life events can precipitate them into further harmful drinking. But if they have already thought about the level of alcohol consumption and are worried about it, that is at the contemplation stage, then the event acts as a trigger, focusing thinking and jolting the individual into doing something about it. Seeking help is one outcome but not everyone will do so. Some people change their drinking behaviour without help. There is much evidence of 'spontaneous remission' from a drinking problem, for example in the work of Saunders and Kershaw (1979) and Tuchfeld's study already discussed. Saunders and Kershaw identified the maintaining factors (Tuchfeld's second significant role for life events) which they found in the sixty 'spontaneous remitters' they studied. Marriage, job change, overall life circumstance change and physical illness were all found to be important. These factors then can exert a positive influence on maintaining a commitment to change. But do life events exert a negative influence on maintaining change, that is are they associated with relapse? Various studies have compared relapsers with non-relapsers, notably Rosenberg (1983) and Billings and Moos (1983). The general consensus, methodological differences notwithstanding, is that relapsers not only experience more negative life events than do non-relapsers, but also experience less positive life events.

Moyra Sidell

Life events and successfully maintaining change

So what part do life events play in maintaining a commitment to change drinking behaviour? Are life events significant in maintaining this commitment?

The relationship between life events and outcome and maintaining that outcome for the problem drinkers studied by Fennell and Sidell (1989) was complicated. There were three main groups. Those who took action to change by seeking treatment and successfully maintained that change for at least two years; those who took action to change and maintained that change for anything between six and eighteen months before relapsing; and those who took action to change by seeking help but did not manage to affect their drinking behaviour significantly.

The lives of all those who successfully maintained change were not characterized by smoothness and tranquillity. On the contrary, many experienced quite stressful life events which did not cause them to relapse. Some brief thumb-nail sketches will best illustrate some of the circumstances with which they had to cope.

Case studies Life events and maintaining change

About six months after undergoing counselling for a drink problem, Mr Briggs, a man in his late fifties, was made redundant. About two months after that, he lost his wife without warning, in quite unnerving circumstances. He had two sons in their early twenties, who both lived at home. One had a regular job but the other was mildly handicapped and able to get only intermittent work. Mr Briggs took on the role of cook-housekeeper and maintained the family with very little money. None of this affected the changes he had made in his drinking behaviour.

Mrs White, whose original drink problem had arisen in reaction to the loss of her teenage son, who was killed in a cycle accident, had sought help through the counselling agency. She had successfully altered her drinking behaviour for about a year when she discovered that her daughter had an incurable blood condition. Although devastated by this news, she did not resort to alcohol because of her previous experience of harmful drinking, which had caused herself and her family a great deal of added pain.

Mrs Williamson had more than her share of misfortune since changing her drinking behaviour. She miscarried her second pregnancy at three months; discovered that her first-born son of one year was totally deaf; lost her father-in-law and had to cope with her husband's severe illness. Finally, she failed her driving test, which was very important to her because her husband worked away and she was isolated with her young child. Although she admits to feeling very upset, particularly at her child's deafness, the life she had carefully built up since her drinking days was far too important for her to jeopardize by drinking heavily and she was all too well aware of the consequences of that behaviour.

Certainly people do learn from their past behaviour. They are not inevitably the passive victims of life events and many gain strength and confidence from having successfully changed their harmful drinking behaviour. But there are some people who are still vulnerable to relapse even though they too have made a commitment to change, taken action by seeking treatment and maintained the change for some time.

Mrs Ross had been in control of her drinking for about eighteen months. Her original drink problem had seriously affected her family life and alienated her husband and teenage daughter. In the eighteen months she had repaired her relationship with her daughter and apparently with her husband. But when she discovered that he was having an affair, her instinct was to get drunk. This she did, but was so frightened by her behaviour that she made further contact with the treatment centre. By being able to talk her problem through with someone she was able to cope with it without reverting to her previous drinking behaviour.

In fact (as discussed more fully in Chapter 5) the whole notion of relapse is somewhat problematic. It assumes a 'back to square one', 'slippery slope' acceptance of 'alcoholic' behaviour. The experience from our study was that no one went from a long period of problem-free drinking to long-term problem drinking once they had taken action to change their behaviour. Others, however, did experience the temporary relapse illustrated by Mrs Ross. But the fact that they were in touch with a helping organization, and had gone through the process successfully before, enabled them to recognize the danger signs and do something about it. It seems important that relapse should not be equated with failure, hopelessness and shame but instead it should as the stages of change model would suggest, be seen as a warning, and the door of treatment agencies left open for people to return to if and when they feel vulnerable.

However, it was certainly not the case that all who sought treatment successfully managed to control their drinking. Some were not successful in changing their drinking behaviour at all. They were still vulnerable to stressful life events and these were frequently consequential to their continued harmful drinking behaviour. In contrast to those who had successfully managed to control their drinking behaviour, this group experienced very few positive life events. This is consistent with other life events research findings that those who do change their drinking behaviour, and manage to maintain that change, experience more positive life events than those who do not successfully maintain that change. And positive life events can certainly help in maintaining changed drinking behaviour. Again, these can be purely fortuitous or actually consequent on the actions taken by the individual, for instance in their relationships.

The whole process of changing drinking behaviour and life-style is likely to affect the occurrence of negative and positive events of the implicated type, such as events surrounding relationships, work, physical health or finances. They act as a measure of the progress made and a reinforcement of that progress, both negatively and positively.

Conclusions

At every stage in a drinking career, life events clearly have an impact on the course of the drinking or the decision to seek help, and on the outcome of treatment. None of these effects is inevitable, and any attempt to be prescriptive about the relationship of life events to any stage in the drinking career would be foolish. It therefore becomes difficult to translate lessons learnt from life events research into models for therapeutic counselling. It seems important to recognize two broad types of life events: those which occur independent of the drinking, and those which are in some way implicated in the drinking. Motivational counselling can help individuals to understand that certain types of life events are consequent upon their drinking behaviour and therefore within their control.

The independent life event seems to affect a small but significant, and mainly female, group of people by precipitating them into heavy or harmful drinking. The implicated life event seems to have a complex interactive effect on the drinking career which can both precipitate the person into further drinking or can act as a trigger to seek help. The implicit hypothesis is that the difference depends on the individual's readiness for change. A stressful life event may, in Prochaska and DiClemente's model, serve to precipitate into further drinking the individual who is at the pre-contemplative stage of readiness to change, whereas a stressful life event may act as a trigger to seek help in the individual who is at a contemplative stage of readiness to change.

However, for many people, deciding to take action to change their behaviour does not mean that they have reached any understanding of their own behaviour or its relation to life events. The contemplation stage may be one of contemplating action; it is not necessarily a stage of contemplation in the sense of looking at one's life and behaviour in any self-analytical sense. People will invariably need help to do this, to look at their drinking and put it in the context of their social and psychological situation in order to understand why they drank harmfully. If this was originally related to stressful life events, then they will need to look at other ways of dealing with such stressful events. They will need support and encouragement to make the necessary changes in their lives. Others will need to think about how their heavy drinking has created stressful situations and events to which they have responded by yet further drinking.

Clearly a prerequisite to motivational counselling is careful assessment of the individual's situation in order to understand the varying needs of those who have reached the stage of action. Life events have to be taken into account and looked at in context and a distinction made between those independent of drinking and those which are in some ways a consequence of heavy drinking. Only by reaching an understanding of why they reacted to certain life events by drinking heavily, and how that heavy drinking might have encouraged further stressful life events, can individuals be enabled to look for other coping mechanisms which will not have the harmful consequences that the heavy consumption of alcohol has had for them in the past.

References

Beckman, L.J. (1975) 'Women alcoholics: a review of social and psychological studies', *Journal of Studies on Alcohol* 36, 7: 797–824.

Billings, A.G. and Moos, R.H. (1983) 'Psychosocial processes of recovery among alcoholics and their families: implications for clinicians and programme evaluators', *Addictive Behaviours* 8: 205–18.

Brown, G.W. and Harris, T. (1978) *The Social Origin of Depression*, London: Tavistock.

Cooke, D.J. and Allan, C.A. (1984) 'Stressful life events and alcohol and alcohol abuse in women: a general population study', *British Journal of Addiction* 79: 425–30.

Dohrenwend, B.S. and Dohrenwend, B.P. (eds) (1974) *Stressful Life Events: Their Nature and Effects*, New York: John Wiley.

Fennell, G. and Sidell, M. (1989) *Social Factors in Problem Drinking – A Longitudinal Study*, University of East Anglia, based on research funded by the Alcohol Education and Research Council.

Holmes, T.H. and Rahe, R.H. (1967) 'The social readjustment rating scale', *Journal of Psychosomatic Research* 11: 213–18.

O'Doherty, F. and Davies, J.B. (1987) 'Life events and addiction: a critical review', *British Journal of Addiction* 82: 127–37.

Paykel, E.S., Myers, J.K. and Dienelt, M.N. with others (1969) 'Life events and depression: a controlled study', *Archives of General Psychiatry* 21: 753–60.

Prochaska, J.O. and DiClemente, C.P. (1984) *The Transtheoretical Approach: Crossing Traditional Boundaries of Therapy*, New York: Daw-Jones Irwin.

Rosenberg, H. (1983) 'Relapsed versus non-relapsed alcohol abusers: coping skills, life events and social support', *Addictive Behaviours* 8: 183–6.

Saunders, W.M. and Kershaw, P.W. (1979) 'Spontaneous remission from alcoholism: a community study', *British Journal of Addiction* 74: 251–65.

Tuchfeld, B.S. (1981) 'Spontaneous remission in alcoholics', *Journal of Studies on Alcohol* 42: 626–41.

Chapter nine

Community services
A motivational approach

Ian MacEwan

Introduction

In most parts of the world enormous changes are occurring in the
organization and financing of health care services. Cost contain-
ment has become all important. There is an increasing expectation
by funders that alcohol services must show identifiable benefits or
positive outcomes. They look to reduced consumption levels within
the general population (often in spite of increased availability),
lower alcohol-related crime statistics, earlier and shorter treatment
interventions, fewer alcohol-related in-patients in hospital beds.
Rather than relying on the alcohol services' own audits and
evaluations, it is likely that funders will increasingly judge for
themselves whether alcohol services are able to deliver. It won't be
easy for government agencies, employers, insurance companies,
local and health authorities to make these judgements; indeed, they
may encourage elements in the preventive and treatment community that are vigorous and sincere yet ineffective and perhaps
harmful. Everywhere, politicians are calling for improvement to the
quality of health care while continuing the commitment to reducing
health care costs.

Most alcohol counsellors are conscientious, dedicated and hard-
working. They genuinely believe in what they are doing. However,
merely examining clients who complete a programme and noting
improvements over their former status proves nothing. Improvement compared to what? To ask less should be insufficient to meet
funding obligations and is insufficient to meet responsibilities to
clients. It will be the intention of this chapter to look at the
implications for service planning of the nature of that improvement, implications which acknowledge the variety of drinking
problems which people present and the variety of their individual
characteristics.

The conceptual approach being taken in this chapter contains:

1 A philosophical commitment to identify needs which are not currently being met and which can be by using the stages of change model (Prochaska and DiClemente 1984).
2 A commitment to early problem identification and treatment, which is clearly invited by this model.
3 The utilization of the model which, with proper resource levels, should result in the reduction of alcohol problem prevalence within a district.

Treatment services

The historical development of services has been generally abstinence based, providing for clients at the action stage. The last ten years have seen a growth in the variety of treatment models and in treatment goals and many services, while still continuing to target clients at the action stage, do also provide counselling and support at other stages, for example, the partners and families of pre-contemplators. A special development of recent years, especially with the non-statutory alcohol advisory service, is a comprehensive agency endeavouring a continuum of primary through tertiary prevention. Alcohol and drug services often seem overwhelmed by the size of the problem and by the competing claims not only of their constituencies within the processes of change but also of the needs of different cultural and social groups experiencing drinking problems.

By using the stages of change model we could start by reviewing the current pattern of services which identify, assess and intervene in problem drinking.

Pre-contemplators

Interventions

Information, education, prevention, harm reduction, primary care training – recognition and assessment, young offenders, drink driving.

Appropriate agencies

Alcohol advisory services, probation, general practitioners, hospitals, health centres, general advice agencies, court workers, government, social services.

Contemplators

Interventions

Primary care training, harm reduction, motivational interviewing, easy or immediate access to treatment, family therapy, physical testing, detoxification.

Appropriate agencies

Alcohol advisory services, probation, general practitioners, social services, family services, advice and counselling agencies, hospitals, health centres, detoxification units.

Changers (people in action stage)

Interventions

Behavioural interventions, counselling, groupwork, residential care, detoxification.

Appropriate agencies

Alcohol advisory services, alcohol treatment units, addictions units, rehabilitation hostels.

Maintainers

Interventions

Life skills, social skills, befriending, relapse-prevention, relapse management, appropriate long-term and open-ended support.

Appropriate agencies

Alcohol advisory services, Alcoholics Anonymous.

Such splitting up of interventions and services into these four categories should not be rigid and there can be overlap. For example, relapse-prevention is often an intervention at the action stage and often provided by such agencies as addiction units and they indeed may also provide an ongoing support group for maintainers.

There are four main types of service treatment: alcohol treatment units, rehabilitation hostels or half-way houses, alcohol advisory services and detoxification services. The trend in service development (wider than just the substance abuse field) is to look towards the comprehensive service providing the interventions listed above and packaged within either of two structures: a single organization providing from primary to tertiary prevention, as in the Councils on Alcohol, or a network of services providing a co-ordinated effort in a particular geographical area. Such an agency or network, modelling its service on the stages of change, will provide for individuals varying in the stage and degree of seriousness of the problem.

The development of such specialized provision must not preclude the parallel development of other primary care services to alcohol-related problems. Social services, health services, court and justice systems and general advice agencies can be effective interveners in the early stages and especially well placed to raise alcohol use matters with pre-contemplators. Breaking down the barriers to involvement by non-specialist agencies invites a more critical look at the distinction between treatment and prevention.

The merging of prevention and treatment

An implication of the stages of change model is that treatment and prevention are not always separate activities. People can sometimes be at more than one stage, for example, the client receiving help for reducing consumption and at the same time being made aware of the risks of trouble due to drinking and how to prevent them. Treatment and prevention can merge into a single activity.

If intervening in problem drinking is as much about education as it is about treatment, then there is a logic to synthesizing programmes directed at managing or preventing dependency. This evolves from the need to address the whole person, often referred to as the holistic approach; it acknowledges the person's movement backwards and forwards along a continuum of alcohol use; it unites the individual, group, community and political elements of alcohol-related problems, and it emphasizes skills development and growth rather than a diagnostic labelling of an individual as 'alcoholic'. Agencies which have moved, and others currently doing so, toward a humanistic education intervention argue for the potential for growth and the need for further development of specific skill areas. Rather than an agency seeing its clients, and therefore they seeing themselves as sick, ill, criminal or deviant, the humanistic milieu provides for client involvement in selecting goals and the methods for achieving them. It responds positively and sympathetically to the individual's process through the stages of change by providing a variety of insights and skills leading toward self-sufficiency rather than a two-dimension drinking – recovered or ill–well polarity.

Planning for alcohol services

A major implication of the Prochaska and DiClemente model (1984) is the need for an expansion both in the kinds of interventions for alcohol-related problems and in the range of individuals for whom interventions are directed. In the diversification of interventions there is likely to be a decline of traditional emphases for example, on medical detoxification and increasing emphases placed on prevention measures and specialized programmes such as those for drinking drivers, which combine aspects of both prevention and treatment. There needs to be better targeting of potential client groups so that as wide a range as possible of people with problems can be reached. Black and Asian people, elderly people, lesbians and gay men, youth, rurally isolated people, all of whom have been under-served, need to be the target of more vigorous planning and out-reach efforts.

Better targeting will focus attention on the allocations of resources based on need. As the primary institutional force, government must take up the leadership role in alcohol research, policy-setting and helping to shape the form of interventions and attendant planning measures. As with other far-reaching public health problems, such as drug abuse and AIDS, the resources necessary to mitigate alcohol problems have been too large for any entity other than central government to underwrite. Local government agencies and regional and district health authorities have been incapable and/or unwilling to support the full costs of research, prevention and interventions necessary to reduce alcohol problems.

In the UK, for example, the current instrument for providing seeding money is Alcohol Concern, but that is only for the use of non-statutory initiatives. Attempts have been made by Alcohol Concern to get each regional health authority to submit a plan documenting what attempts were being made to assess alcohol-related problems and what prevention and treatment services were in place to meet these problems. The results showed idiosyncratic development and uneven distribution of services.

The planning process

The limited amount of funds a region has available for alcohol programmes must be distributed so as to best meet the needs of populations within the region. Questions of equity and efficiency inform this process. For efficiency most funds will often be directed to districts with the highest concentration of people and where the most return is provided for the investment made. The larger districts would thus get more resources and smaller districts less, but the total resources for both large and small districts in a regional health authority, must be pooled to establish an equity in their availability to all people within that particular region. Thus, for instance, an individual in a rural district may have to travel to an adjoining urban district where a greater variety of treatment services have been established in order to serve the larger population more efficiently, but that rural dweller is guaranteed ability to obtain the same services available to the urban dweller, this availability being a product of the recognition of equity and regional health organization.

In some regions, planning may be done on a strictly district level but this is more likely to be the case where the district populations are so large as to ensure that both criteria of equity and efficiency are met when planning for individual districts.

When addressing the issues of efficiency and equity, there are several factors which must be considered and appear particularly important when planning a district-based alcohol service.

1 *Clients* Pre-contemplators, contemplators, the determined, maintainers.
2 *Interventions* How many and what types of primary, secondary and tertiary services will and should be used?
3 *Resources* What is the need and who is best able to provide for it?
4 *Location* Where should the services be offered to ensure that they will be accessible?
5 *Pattern of service* How should the services be offered – in what kinds of settings and by what kinds of organizational structures?

We shall now look at these factors more closely.

Clients

In the alcohol service field, most of the publicly funded programmes have traditionally served a low-income client group, many in receipt of Social Security benefits. However, if our services are to be truly comprehensive, they should explore the needs of all residents in their catchment, irrespective of current and past client groups. Services need to be marketed to the pre-contemplator, the contemplator and the maintainer. Marketing a service solely to those committed to the action stage risks poor take-up, especially from those groups who do not utilize the services presently. Failure to do this not only means ignoring the needs of people at different stages of change but also means continuing to under-service particular groups who are under-represented in our client statistics. It is not enough simply to hang one's shingle out and await an unending line of customers. High-risk groups within the community must be identified and targeted: youth, women, elderly people, certain occupation groups, lesbians, gay men, social and ethnic minorities.

Groups with a high prevalence of alcohol-related problems need first to be reached in terms of their group social behaviour, norms and values in relation to alcohol use. Responding to the needs of individuals without trying to change the social context in which they operate may often end in the fruitless task of persuading individual people not to want what they do want and to want what they do not. In essence, the targeted population must see the new moderate drinking goal as being desirable and the proper service as being credible before it will support the take-up of that service by its members. In alcohol treatment planning, competition among several programmes in the same geographic area for the same potential clients is generally viewed as an inefficient use of public (and private) funds. A specific programme should be assigned to serve a particular client group within each district. In developing and sustaining programmes, need should be documented. Decisions to develop new services should be made only after documentation of problem prevalence, presence of particular client groups, consideration of appropriate interventions and evaluation of the proposed development plan.

Interventions

Our client population should be seen in terms of four groups with differing characteristics, needs and requiring various responses: pre-contemplators, contemplators, changers and maintainers.

Pre-contemplators

People who are unaware of the harmful pattern of their substance use, or who perhaps are aware but are not willing as yet to do anything about it: these form the majority of our client population. They can be reached through information and education, prevention and health promotion, primary care training, work with young offenders and with drunken drivers. Probation, health and social welfare workers can be trained in identification, assessment and early intervention, and be providers of information. A voluntary sector alcohol and drugs advice service operating from a shop-front can be an effective informer and intervener.

Contemplators

People who are aware of problems in their lives and that alcohol or other substance is mixed up in them. Maybe they want to do something but don't know how or where to go or what the options might be. Perhaps they know that some action is needed but they feel uncommitted or unprepared. One might call them 'The

Unsure', the next largest part of the client population. Primary care training, harm-reduction work, motivational interviewing, easy or immediate access to early intervention workers, family therapy, physical testing or detoxification are all responses appropriate to this stage. Contemplators often need a non-medical advice service easily accessible and with the minimum of bureaucratic procedures. However, an intervention can be effected with in-patients of hospital services by staff who have received even a little training. Over 40 per cent of people who determine upon changing their substance use will do so, given a little information and support (Roizen *et al.* 1978).

Changers

These people are 'The Determined'. They are embarked upon action on their substance-use problems. Behavioural interventions, counselling, groupwork, residential care or detoxification may be needed. It is only a small group who need an intensive intervention. Yet traditionally, services have been geared towards this group exclusively.

Maintainers

People who, having created the change with their substance use, now maintain the new pattern. Life skills, social skills, befriending, relapse-prevention and management, availability of long-term and open-ended support. Alcoholics Anonymous is, for some, an effective provider in this area.

Resources

The approach taken in this chapter does assume a relatively steady wider acceptance of

1 public policies which encourage the moderate use of alcohol and treatment for alcohol-related problems
2 people's attitudes about the desirability of treatment for alcohol-related problems
3 the availability of public funding
4 the level of targeting and out-reach by the agency.

The planning difficulty is getting the right level of service (including staff, facilities, therapeutic hours and number of bed spaces) to match the incidence and prevalence of alcohol-related problems in the district. In setting this goal, it is necessary to establish a level of effective treatment intervention, specifying the estimated resources required to achieve a desired standard.

Though not such a problem in the UK as elsewhere, the temptation by funders to mushrooming development (fund any new agency applicant with a good idea), apart from other considerations as to its merit, leaves all agencies starved of funds, especially in times of zero-budgeting. It is a much better use of resources to invest funds in existing agencies with a good record of effective programme administration and tag the funding, if necessary, to be used for special targeting purposes. Rather than encouraging new agencies to get started, where possible it must be better to encourage existing well-run agencies to identify and provide for need.

Location

Having defined which interventions should be available within a region, decisions must be made on optimal location. For services which are used only periodically or for short stays, a wide dispersal of service locations may be most efficient. For example, the location chosen for a detoxification facility will not be as much a function of the availability of public transport as that of out-patient clinics or counselling centres. The location issue, however, will more often revolve around the total absence of a service within an area. Frequently the need will have been triggered by the demands of a citizens' group representing an unserved geographical area.

Standards of geographic coverage may vary considerably, depending upon the relative ruralness or urbanness of the area. During the 1970s and early to mid-1980s a public policy was commonly based on the theory that the inner-city neighbourhood was an optimal service area, particularly neighbourhoods which contained high concentrations of low-income people. However, the efficiency of the neighbourhood concept service must be weighed against other concepts which take cost, travel time and convenience to potential clients into consideration. A travel time of an hour or so may be routine in rural areas; but in older cities, people's entire regimen of work, leisure and family may centre around a borough. These local variations in life-styles must be taken into account in assessing the best location for service delivery.

Patterns of service

Organization, for agencies, has the underlying goal of providing services with efficiency. The stages of change model, by identifying the client's stage in the process and so the better delivery of a selected intervention, can mean choices between several alternative combinations of services, the elimination of unnecessary duplication of services and the estimation of the number and type of staff who will deliver effectively at the primary, secondary or tertiary levels.

The stages of change model identifies the specific agencies, or programmes and staff within agencies, which should most appropriately deliver any particular service (see example below). In doing so, there are a number of practical organizational issues, such as the willingness of clients to use a given agency, as well as the potential for integration of a new client group within the programme structure in the agency. In essence, organizational questions involve sifting of various alternative auspices for service delivery, with the objective of providing an effective service in the most efficient manner.

Aspects of organizational melancholia often cited by agency staffs include poor treatment outcome, lack of clear policy and direction, early termination of treatment by clients, lack of an understanding of process, manipulative clients, lack of a treatment philosophy informing practice.

These can be addressed by careful consideration of the stages of change. While the complexity of the task being undertaken must be recognized and agency staff need look at themselves and their colleagues in terms of competence as practitioners and at the organizational structure in force, it is to the pattern of service that the model is especially pertinent.

Setting up a community service: an example

The example given here will take the form of a basic blueprint which can be built upon or adapted as need requires.

The principle

A comprehensive, patient-effective, cost-effective alcohol and drugs service providing for people at the four stages of change: pre-contemplation, contemplation, action and maintenance.

Proposal

A comprehensive alcohol and drugs service to prevent alcohol and drug abuse, and to deal with its consequences including those who have alcohol-related and drug-related problems.

Strategic elements

1 The prevention of alcohol and drug misuse including health promotion and public education initiatives.
2 Work-place policies adopted by employers and employees to reduce alcohol and drug misuse at the work-place and to help those who develop problems.
3 Education and training of primary care workers such as doctors, nurses and social workers to tackle alcohol and drug problems as part of their normal work.
4 Community-based services for problem drinkers and their families covering individual counselling, groupwork, day centre programmes, as well as advice and self-help manuals.
5 Culturally appropriate responses for minority groups determined by planners from those groups.

These activities are best carried out at different levels. Some services are best provided within each district; this is where the service needs to be close to the user and integrated into existing primary care networks. Other services should be at a multi-district level in the interests of economies of scale and efficient co-ordination. Some functions are best carried out at a regional level where strategic planning and monitoring require an overview to be taken.

District health authority/voluntary sector

The services outlined can be provided by either the health authority or a voluntary sector body. If both are used, they should work in partnership with an agreed strategy and each should be clear about the other's role. If a voluntary sector body is carrying out the work, it should be properly funded. It could be that a service contract is worked out between the health authority and the voluntary agency. This enables the authority to retain its responsibility while delegating the work to the voluntary agency but within clear guidelines. The strength of the voluntary sector includes its non-medical model of delivery, its ability to be flexible and innovative as well as its capacity to attract additional funds.

Model of service provision

Table 9.1 is a proposal for developing a response to alcohol and drug problems in a district. It is proposed as a minimum for the development of an adequate service. Particularly in new areas of work they may need to be revised upwards as experience is gained.

Table 9.1 Proposed model of service provision

Task	No of staff	Duties
Pre-contemplators and contemplators	1 Health promotion worker	Information, public education and awareness-raising
	1 Trainer	Training of GPs, social workers, clergy, nurses, occupational counsellors, school counsellors, and so on
	1 Employee Assistance Programme (EAP) worker	To work with the EAP scheme developing alcohol policies in the work-place
Changers	3 Counsellors/group workers	Working with problem drinkers and their families
Maintainers	N Volunteers	Befriending
	1 Manager (if appropriate, a minority group development worker)	
	1 Secretary/receptionist	

Other services

Where in-patient detoxification is needed, the hospitals can provide this care. Residential provision is now widely available and it is probably not necessary to create more.

Needs of black and ethnic minority people

The model proposed is hopefully trans-cultural but can be adapted easily to fit cultural needs. The development worker is essentially that and it is not suggested that this person is THE response to alcohol and drug problems within ethnic communities. The whole agency should reflect the ethnic proportions in the district and be committed to a multi-cultural perspective.

Developing an effective service

By dividing its target population into four groups

1 unwilling to consider change
2 unsure about change
3 determined upon change
4 maintaining change

the scene is set for the consideration of four elements of developing an effective service: the compiling of a mission statement, developing an agency or unit praxis, addressing issues of competence and developing the culture of the agency.

Mission statement

The first element is the compiling of a *mission statement.* An idea used by business organizations for many years, it has recently been taken up by some public sector agencies as a brief, single-sentence statement which expresses the mission of the agency. It can then act as the standard against which all practice, ideas and development can be measured. It can act as a rallying call and as a unifying factor, enabling agencies to act with a common single purpose. The mission statement for Otis Elevators is 'to move people horizontally and vertically over short distances'. That is the Otis mission: all work and all innovations must be loyal to that statement. How many alcohol services agencies have headed off in several directions and, as a consequence, lost a sense of purpose? The Wellington (New Zealand) Alcohol and Drug Centre has a mission statement. Theirs is in three sentences but the idea is apparent:

> To provide an accessible professional specialist assessment service for people with alcohol and drug problems, and those affected by them, within the Wellington Area Health Board.
> To formulate and offer individually appropriate out-patient treatment and referral to other agencies, with follow-up for both.
> We will continue to use a sensitive multi-cultural approach.

Like a treaty, it is a standard against which individual, organizational and practical issues can be measured.

Unit praxis

The second step is the developing of a *unit praxis.*

1 Why are we doing it?
2 What do we want to achieve?
3 Who are we serving?
4 Are there people missing out?
5 Are we providing for pre-contemplators, contemplators and maintainers?
6 Can we be an agency of excellence?
7 A role model?

Issues of competence

The third step in this specific process is to address *issues of competence.* It is crucial for staff to believe in their own competence and in the competence of their co-workers. Competence can be addressed, promoted and monitored by good supervision that is regular, relevant and provided by experienced and trusted workers.

Agency culture

Agency culture is the social context in which the staff behave and relate: a pattern of accepted habits, values and rules.

1 Who has the authority? Clearly set out the line of decision-making responsibility.
2 What are the values? It is important to clarify and set out the agency's beliefs and principles. Not only is it important for funders, referrers and other strategic organizations but also it is important for the maintenance of staff cohesion and purpose. Is there a disparity between the values of the agency and its practice?
3 What are the norms? These might be the standards for behaviour and expectations on staff, e.g. sharing information, helping one another, collective problem-solving.
4 What are the rewards? Reward is an essential ingredient of good team-work and for building morale: build in rewards from the staff night out to time off and from study leave to promotion and pay rises. Caring services are not always very good at rewarding hard work.
5 What are the sanctions? This is the opposite side of the coin. How is poor work or lack of interest managed? Team morale is as dependent upon the exercise of sanctions as it is upon reward.
6 How appropriate is this culture to the success of a particular programme, the agency, or the client group?

Staff may be experiencing alienation by lacking an identification with agency purpose, so as to be not contributing but just working; enduring conflict and antagonism between staff, perhaps working at cross-purposes; suffering despair, with feelings of discouragement and disheartenment; settling into mediocrity, with staff not bothering much anymore and doing just enough not to be sanctioned.

These kinds of problems are part of the agency culture and can be addressed in the context of whether or not the problems are individual to one or more staff members, organizational to the whole agency or practical to the treatment programme.

Summary

If current trends continue, funding in the future may well be allocated to those services which can clearly demonstrate results achieved rather than services provided. Results achieved means not only reduced prevalence of problems but also clients who are dependent upon alcohol regaining control. The preceding chapters have suggested ways in which by using the stages of change model and by using techniques such as motivational interviewing better results can be achieved. This chapter has enquired into how the model might influence service planning.

It is important when dealing constructively with the factors of client groups, interventions, resources, pattern of services and location to situate them, and the effective and efficient service development towards which they are directed, in the proper real-world perspective. Therefore, those factors should be considered in the light of two questions.

1 What has been the past and what is the current problem and service situation?
2 What should the future pattern of service be?

Valid and reliable ways of helping people to change cannot be conducted in an historical vacuum. Placing those factors discussed above in a context of that which is past and that which is current should be seen as prologue. Much can be done to generate information about the problem in both directions: past and future. In this way, it will be possible to develop an understanding of how problems behave across time, and assessments can be made concerning the impact of pre-contemplation, contemplation, action and maintenance delivery systems on the problems.

References

Prochaska, J.O. and DiClemente, C.C. (1984) *The Transtheoretical Approach: Crossing Traditional Boundaries of Therapy*, New York: Daw-Jones Irwin.

Roizen, R., Cahalan, D. and Shanks, P. (1978) 'Spontaneous remission among untreated problem drinkers', in D. Kandel (ed.) *Longitudinal Research on Drug Use: Empirical Findings and Methodological Issues*, Washington, DC: Hemisphere.

Name index

Subject index

Subject index